REAL KIDS
REAL ADVENTURES

REAL KIDS REAL ADVENTURES

TRUE STORIES BY DEBORAH MORRIS

RUNAWAY BALLOON!

RESCUE IN THE TRINITY RIVER

APARTMENT INFERNO!

BROADMAN
& HOLMAN
PUBLISHERS

Nashville, Tennessee

Published by
Broadman & Holman Publishers
Nashville, Tennessee

Design: Steven Boyd

Printed in the United States of America

4240-53
0-8054-4053-4

Dewey Decimal Classification: JSC
Subject Heading:
Adventure and adventurers\Lifesaving—Stories, plots, etc.
Library of Congress Card Catalog Number: 94-11741

Library of Congress Cataloging-in-Publication Data

Morris, Deborah, 1956–
    Real kids, real adventures / by Deborah Morris.
        p. cm.
    ISBN 0-8054-4053-4
    1. Christian biography—United States—Juvenile literature.
2. Children—United States—Biography—Juvenile litera-
ture.   3. Survival.   4. Adventure and adventurers.
5. Christian biography.   I. Title.
    BR1714.M67   1994
    209'.2'273—dc20
    94-11741
    [B]   CIP
    AC

ISBN 0-8054-4051-8 (vol. 1)
ISBN 0-8054-4053-4 (vol. 3)

To my grumpy friend, Jay Gaines,
who listens to me even when nobody else will.

The "Yellow Rose of Tex's" flies across the Colorado Sky.

Runaway Balloon

The Alex Nicholos Story

Alex frowned, his dark eyebrows knit with concentration as he worked a small screwdriver along the back of his mom's broken clock. She probably expected the clock to end up like everything else he tried to "fix"—stored in one of the many boxes of tangled wires and screws stacked around his room. But this time he was hopeful. How hard could it be to figure out a little alarm clock?

He wiggled the edge of the screwdriver into the plastic casing and twisted it, making the back pop off.

1

The sturdy eleven-year-old was a natural-born "tinkerer." He loved finding out how things worked. A whole string of old toasters, hair dryers, and radios had made their way into his bedroom never to toast, dry, or play again. But with each new project he had learned something. Someday, he was sure, he'd be able to put all that knowledge to good use!

Alex spread the pieces of the clock out on the floor, careful not to pull any wires loose. His basement bedroom in the ranch-style house looked more like a messy workshop than anything else, but Alex liked it that way. It was hard to see his carpet for the jumble of parts, Construx blocks, and small motors lying around, but he knew exactly where to find every part he needed.

"OK," he said to himself as he touched the clock's circuit board with the screwdriver, "what's the problem here?" His mom had said the numbers just suddenly blinked out. The wiring looked OK, so it had to be something wrong with the electronics. He wished he knew what all the little microchips did.

Shrugging, Alex poked around with the tip of his screwdriver and wiggled a few wires. When he plugged in the clock to see what happened, he was amazed to see the numbers light up. They were flashing "12:00."

"Hey, Mom!" he yelled. He put the clock back down on the floor and ran out to call up the basement stairs. "Mom! Come here! I fixed your clock!"

His mother, Linda Nicholos, a slender woman with curly brown hair, appeared at the top of the stairs. "You fixed it?" she asked in surprise. "Really?"

"Really! Come see for yourself!"

Trotting down the stairs, Mrs. Nicholos went into Alex's room, wading carefully through all the stuff scattered on the floor. She picked up the clock, holding the loose parts together to examine it.

"Well," she said admiringly, "I'm impressed. How'd you do it?"

Alex shrugged sheepishly. "I dunno," he admitted. "I just sort of poked around with the screwdriver and it started working again."

"Well, good job. A patient finally survived the operation, huh?"

"I guess so. Got anything else you need fixed?"

Mrs. Nicholos laughed. "Nope. But maybe now that you're on a roll you can put some of these," she swept her arm across the room, taking in all the broken appliances, "back together again."

It was a cold Saturday morning, the first weekend in January. Alex and his nine-year-old sister, Stephanie, had enjoyed every minute of their Christmas break from Penrose Elementary.

Alex's favorite Christmas gift was his new red sled. The city of Colorado Springs, although ringed with mountain peaks, didn't often get a good snowfall. This weekend, however, there was a little snow on the ground.

Alex screwed the clock back together, thinking he might as well go outside and enjoy the snow before it melted away. Maybe Jeff could come over later that afternoon.

Sure enough, by that afternoon the snow was gone. Alex's best friend, Jeff, rode over. They cruised the neighborhood together, Alex on his skateboard-scooter, Jeff on his bike. They talked and laughed, trying not to think too much about school starting again on Monday.

The only good thing about it, Alex thought, would be that he'd get to see Jennifer again. With her long brown hair and bright smile, Jennifer almost made up for math and English classes.

Jeff noticed Alex's sudden silence. "Why are you so quiet?" he demanded.

Alex, startled, blinked in the chilly air. "Uh, just thinking about school," he said quickly. "Hey, Jeff, did I show you this?" Pumping his scooter along with one foot, he moved ahead of his friend. "Watch the back of my scooter!"

The skateboard with a tall scooter handle attached was another one of Alex's "projects." He had wrapped chicken wire around the back edge of the skateboard and then bent some of it down so it would drag along the concrete. When he went fast, it made sparks. It looked great.

"Cool!" Jeff said. "I bet that'll look *really* cool at night!"

"Yeah. That's what I thought."

They spent the afternoon going back and forth between their houses, picking up snacks at both places. It took a lot of energy—and food—to stay warm when it was freezing outside. When they got back to Alex's house late that afternoon, they decided to take a break and watch some television.

Mr. Nicholos, in the kitchen, waved to them cheerfully as they tramped through. After working all week as a psychologist, George Nicholos found it relaxing to do the cooking on weekends. That night supper was going to be Alex's favorite—spaghetti and meatballs.

"So," Jeff said as he plopped down on the couch, "what are you gonna do tomorrow? It's our last day of freedom before school starts!"

Alex groaned. "I wish Christmas break lasted three whole months, like summer. But tomorrow's going to be a lot of fun. A friend of my mom's, a guy named Tex Houston, asked if our family could come crew for him when he takes his hot air balloon up in the morning. He needs some help unloading his trailer and setting up the balloon."

"Sounds like fun. Do you get to take a ride?"

"I don't think so. Mom says that sometimes when you crew for a pilot they invite you along for the ride, but if Tex takes anybody it'll probably be Mom. He's in one of her classes at college."

"That's lousy. Then why go help him?"

Alex shrugged. "I dunno. I've never seen a hot air balloon up close, so it'll probably be interesting. I've always wondered how they work."

Jeff laughed. "You gonna take it apart while nobody's looking? Maybe bring some parts home for your collection?"

Mrs. Nicholos interrupted them by calling: "Dinnertime!" She stuck her head around the corner into the living room. "Jeff, it's time for you to head on home. Alex, go wash your hands and get your sister."

Alex sighed. "See you later, Jeff. I'll call you tomorrow after we get back, OK?"

Over dinner, Alex asked a lot of questions about hot air balloons. His mom knew a little about them from talking to Tex.

"Balloons are a lot bigger than they look when they're up in the sky," she said. "And they're also a lot heavier. Tex says it takes three or four people to unload the balloon and spread it out on the ground so it can get inflated. That's what we're going to do."

Mr. Nicholos asked, "What time are we supposed to be out at the field?"

"You'll love this. He wants us there at six o'clock in the morning. You'll be the only one awake at that hour. We'll all have to jump out of bed and go straight over there. Maybe afterwards we can eat breakfast at Denny's."

"Denny's?" Stephanie chimed in. "Good! I like eating there."

Off to the Launch

The next morning, when Alex's alarm went off at five-thirty, he could hardly open his eyes. Then he remembered that they were launching Tex's balloon that morning. He jumped up and peeled off his pajamas, and then reached for his glasses so he could what he was doing.

After burrowing through his drawers for warm clothes and socks, he pulled them on quickly. It was dark and cold outside, and the open field would be windy. His mom had said to bundle up.

He finally grabbed his thick winter jacket and gloves and pulled a blue stocking cap over his uncombed hair. Why bother combing his hair if he was just going to crunch it under a hat? His mom, for some reason, never understood that. She made him comb his hair every morning, no matter what. This time of day, though, she'd probably be too sleepy to notice.

He climbed the basement stairs and went into the kitchen. His mom and dad were drinking coffee and urging Stephanie to get her shoes on. Stephanie's long brown hair was tangled, and she was rubbing her eyes and looking confused. Alex thought about teasing her, but she was *really* grumpy in the mornings. He decided to leave her alone.

"You ready to go?" Mrs. Nicholos asked, spotting him.

"Yeah," Alex said. He wasn't exactly cheerful in the mornings either.

."Then let's head out. We don't want to be late."

Tex and five other pilots planned to launch their balloons in a big open field about fifteen minutes from their house. When the Nicholoses drove up they saw Tex sitting in his Suburban. It had a box-like white trailer hooked onto the back and a clear plastic strip attached to the front that said: "The Yellow Rose of Tex's."

Mrs. Nicholos laughed. "'Yellow Rose' is the name of his balloon. That's pretty funny . . . you know, like the song, 'The Yellow Rose of Texas.'"

Alex and Stephanie looked at each other with puzzled expressions. Their parents always seemed to know the weirdest songs.

As soon as their car stopped Alex jumped out. It looked like they were some of the first ones there. Tex got out of his car and crunched across the snow-dotted field to meet them. He was a short, plump man with thick glasses and a gray beard, and he was bundled up like Santa Claus.

"Well, this must be the Nicholos family!" Tex said with a big smile. "I really appreciate you folks coming out like this to help."

"This is exciting for all of us," Mrs. Nicholos admitted. "The kids have never seen a hot air balloon up close. Oh, you remember my husband, George. And these are our kids, Alex and Stephanie."

Tex nodded. "Nice to meet you," he said. "Well, I guess we should go ahead and start unloading. It's going to take longer than usual to get set up. My balloon was in the shop last week and I have to reattach the skirt."

Stephanie looked at Mrs. Nicholos. "The *skirt?*" she whispered. Mrs. Nicholos smiled and shrugged. "Guess it's a balloon part," she whispered back.

Alex followed Tex over to the back of the balloon trailer and watched curiously as he opened the large swing-down door. Inside were several boxes and bags, a fan attached to a pull-start engine, and a large wicker balloon basket.

"Wow," said Alex, his eyes wide.

"OK, first we need to get all this stuff out of the trailer and just set it down here on the grass," Tex said. "Linda, could I get you and Stephanie to go over the ground in this area," he pointed with his hand, indicating a large grassy area, "and clear away all the sharp rocks and sticks? We're going to spread the envelope out on the ground over there, and I don't want it to get snagged."

Alex was listening. "Is the envelope the balloon part?" he asked.

"That's right," Tex said. "The part that fills with air."

Alex followed his dad and Tex into the small trailer. They had to bend over to keep from banging their heads.

"Alex, grab the back corner of the basket," Mr. Nicholos said. "If we each take a corner it shouldn't be too hard."

The basket, or "gondola," was much heavier than it looked. With some difficulty they lugged it out of the trailer. Alex stood on tiptoe to peer down into the basket.

The top edge, padded with brown leather, came up to his shoulders. Two bulky metal tanks were strapped in opposite corners, and there was a red fire extinguisher and a CB radio. There was also a square hole in the side of the basket.

Alex leaned down to stick his hand through it. "What's this for?" he asked, wiggling his hand. "Is it like a porthole or something?"

Tex laughed. "It's a step. It makes it easier to climb into the basket."

"Oh." Alex was still storing that information away when his mom yelled, "Alex! Don't start pestering Tex with a million questions. We've got a lot of work to do!"

The sun was rising, sending a harsh, slanting glare across the field. Alex reluctantly tore himself away to go help his dad drag out the thick canvas bag that contained the balloon.

Tex opened the bag and grabbed an edge of the bright yellow fabric. "OK," he said, "now it's time to streamer the envelope. That's where we spread it out on the ground so I can hook everything up to it."

Tex grabbed an edge of the balloon and started walking backward, tugging it along with him. Alex and Stephanie did the same. Alex was surprised at how heavy the fabric felt. He'd somehow pictured a balloon as much lighter.

"That's good!" Tex finally shouted. The envelope, once it was spread out, was a full seventy-five feet long. "Now it'll just take me a few minutes to hook up the skirt."

In the field around them, the other pilots and crews had arrived and were busy setting up their own balloons. Alex trotted back over to watch Tex. He saw why the part was called a skirt. It was made of the same yellow fabric as the balloon, and it was shaped just like a girl's skirt. One end was held open by something that looked like a big hulahoop. The other end was loose and had a bunch of straps dangling from it.

"What's that for?" Alex asked.

Tex was looping the straps, one by one, through metal rings sewn inside the balloon. "It's like a windscreen," he explained. "It hangs down around the burners to keep the wind from blowing out the pilot light."

"Where do the burners go? How do they work?"

"You'll see in just a minute. These propane tanks here," he tapped one of the metal tanks inside the basket, "carry fuel. The two burners hang just above your head. Whenever you want to go higher you pull this cord, and flames shoot right up into the balloon, heating the air. Since hot air rises, that's what pushes you up."

"I know. I learned about that in science." Alex was silent for a moment, thinking. "I guess you can't really steer a hot air balloon, huh?"

"Nope. You go where the wind blows. That's what makes it exciting!"

Alex finally wandered back over to where his mom and dad were waiting. What he wouldn't give for a chance to go up in a balloon like the Yellow Rose!

"Did Tex tell you how everything works?" Mr. Nicholas asked. "Looked like you were really interrogating him."

Alex flushed. "I wasn't bugging him. He liked telling me about all his stuff."

"Just don't pester him too much, OK? You ask an awful lot of questions."

Alex, irritated, walked over to sit down next to Stephanie. He was always getting in trouble for bugging people, but what was wrong with asking a few questions? Would they rather him be stupid?

"Hey, look!" Stephanie said. "The balloon over there is taking off!"

Sure enough, a colorful red, blue, and yellow balloon across the field was slowly rising. Even from where they were sitting they could hear the whooshing sound from the burner. It lifted smoothly into the clear morning sky.

Alex looked around, suddenly realizing that all the other balloons were inflated, ready to take off. The Yellow Rose was going to be the last one to launch.

When Tex finished attaching the skirt it stuck out from the balloon like a short tunnel. Tipping the basket onto its side, Tex hooked it to some steel cables sewn inside the balloon. Then he attached the burners. They dangled in the middle of the "hulahoop" ring.

"OK!" he finally called. "Time to get this show on the road! George, why don't you and Alex grab the crown rope. That's the long line attached at the top. You'll need to walk way out away from the balloon and hang on good and tight to keep the wind from rolling it right over."

He turned to Mrs. Nicholos. "Linda, can you and Stephanie help hold the envelope open? I'm going to use the fan now to pack it with cold air."

After Alex disappeared with the crown line, Dave Hollenbaugh, another balloon pilot, walked up to the group. He helped Tex haul the big fan out of the trailer and then pointed it into the mouth of the balloon. Tex pulled on a helmet and stood next to the tipped-over basket as Mr. Hollenbaugh started the fan.

With a noisy roar, air started rushing into the envelope. The sides of the Yellow Rose gently fluttered and then rounded out. Over the next ten minutes it grew rounder and firmer. Soon the Yellow Rose was towering as high as a four-story building, even though it was still lying on its side.

Tex peered inside the balloon. "Now I need somebody to work their way underneath to unfold the places that are bunched up!" He had to yell to be heard over the fan. "We've still got some wrinkles!"

"I'll do it!" Stephanie called. Mr. Hollenbaugh took her place holding open the balloon as she darted over to the edge. She shoved her way under, bumping along under the smooth fabric like a mouse under a carpet. After straightening the wrinkles, she bumped her way back out into the cold air. "I think I got them all," she said, flipping her hair out of her face. "That was fun!"

"You did a good job," Tex said with satisfaction. "I think we can start giving it some heat now."

Stephanie took her place again at the mouth of the balloon, and Mr. Hollenbaugh walked over to turn down the fan. Tex aimed the burners sideways into the mouth of the balloon and then pulled the cord. With a loud "whoosh" and a burst of heat, twelve-foot flames shot past Mrs. Nicholos and Stephanie into the middle of the balloon.

"Yow!" Stephanie exclaimed, "That's really hot!" The Yellow Rose straightened a little, angling the basket up with it.

Whoosh! Another noisy burst of flame, and the Yellow Rose straightened even more. Tex stepped into the basket.

"OK, Dave, go ahead and turn off the fan!" he said. "I need weight on!"

Mr. Hollenbaugh nodded. Motioning to several members of a nearby ground crew to come over, he turned off the big fan and shoved it out of the way. Then he asked Mrs. Nicholos and Stephanie to come over to the basket.

"'Weight on' means we all need to lean on the basket to keep the balloon from getting away till we're ready," he explained. "It gets jumpy right before you launch."

Mrs. Nicholos and Stephanie draped themselves across the basket, trying to be heavy. Mr. Hollenbaugh gathered up the fan and canvas balloon bag and carried them to Tex's trailer to be put away. Everything needed to be loaded up neatly before the balloon launched.

Tex pulled the burner cord once more, making the balloon and basket stand straight up. Alex and Mr. Nicholos walked up, carrying the crown line. Tex tied it loosely to the edge of the basket and then made one last check of his equipment. Everything was in great shape.

Finally Tex looked up. He saw that Stephanie was hanging onto the edge of the basket in front of him, laughing at something Alex had said. The pilot suddenly grinned.

"Hey, Stephanie," he said. "How would you like to go for a quick balloon ride?"

Stephanie's mouth dropped open. She glanced up at the huge balloon overhead and then quickly shook her head. "Uh, no, I don't think so," she said. "Thanks anyway."

Alex, beside her, made a quick movement. He knew his mom and dad would kill him if he asked, but it was all he could do to keep from blurting out, "What about me, Tex?"

As if reading his mind, the pilot looked over at him. "Well, Alex, what about you?"

Alex's whole face lit up with a huge grin. "Sure!" he said. Before Tex could change his mind—and before his mom could stop him—he climbed over into the basket. Tex handed him a helmet and waited as he put it on.

"OK, I guess we're off! Weight off, hands on."

Up, Up and Away

Following the lead of the other ground crews, the Nicholoses eased their bodies off the basket. It hovered just above the ground, steadied by six pairs of hands.

Tex pulled the burner again briefly and then shouted, "Hands off!" Everybody backed away. The balloon shot up off the ground.

"Bye!" Alex yelled, leaning out to wave. "See you later!" He was surprised at how quickly they were rising. It was like being on a fast elevator.

Stephanie waved back. "Bye, Alex!" She looked small, and so did Tex's van and balloon trailer. Alex waved one last time and then turned to look around. They were already high above the treetops!

"This is so-o-o fun!" he said sincerely. "Thanks a lot for bringing me, Mr. Houston. I really wanted to come. I can't believe my sister chickened out."

Tex chuckled. "Just call me Tex, son. Well, you looked like the adventurous type. I thought you might enjoy it."

He pointed ahead to the other five balloons that had launched before them. They were stretched out across the sky to the north, looking like colorful little dots. Tex pulled the burner, boosting the Yellow Rose still higher.

When Alex looked back at the field where they had taken off, he couldn't see his mom and dad anymore. Tex's big Suburban, looking like a Hot Wheels toy, seemed to be moving across the field.

Just then a voice crackled over the radio. "Yellow Rose, this is Yellow Rose Chase. Radio check."

"Yellow Rose Chase, this is Yellow Rose. You're loud and clear."

Alex listened, eyes wide. "Who was that?"

"That's my friend Dave Hollenbaugh, down in the chase vehicle. Didn't you meet him while he was helping us set up?"

"I don't think so. Me and my dad were out holding that rope for a long time."

"Oh, that's right. Well, Dave is a balloon pilot, too. He's probably got your parents and sister with him. See, your ground crew always follows you when you're up in a balloon. They keep you in sight and are waiting right there when you land. Otherwise it'd be a long walk back, right?"

Alex smiled. "Oh, yeah. And I guess you'd have to carry the whole balloon back, too. That wouldn't be much fun." He leaned his elbows on the side of the basket and looked down. Tex's Suburban was following along a narrow road behind them.

Tex checked several small gauges. "What are those for?" Alex asked.

The pilot tapped a narrow instrument. "This one is called a variometer. See this needle? It shows how fast we're going up or down. If it's lying flat to the left, pointing to zero, you're flying level. If it's pointing up to two hundred, you're rising at two hundred feet per minute. If it drops below the zero to two hundred, you're going *down* two hundred feet per minute."

"Cool. And what's that one for?" Alex pointed to a small digital gauge that read: "7200."

"That's the altimeter. It tells how high we are above sea level. Like right now, we're seventy-two hundred feet up. That makes us, oh, about one thousand feet above the ground."

Alex whistled. "That's pretty high. So where do you think we'll end up?"

"Oh, we'll just ride the wind till we find a safe place to land. I'll check with the other balloons here in a minute and see where they're putting down. It feels like the wind is picking up a little, so we may have to make it a short flight."

They drifted along in silence for a few minutes, enjoying the warm sunshine. Snowy fields spread out in every direction beneath the balloon, dotted with occasional houses and other buildings. The only sound that interrupted from time to time was the whoosh of the burner.

Alex glanced forward to the north. The other balloons all seemed to be getting lower in the sky. Tex picked up the radio. "Camelot, this is Yellow Rose. You guys find a good spot to put down?"

"Camelot. I've already ripped out over here by the high school. The wind's getting rough . . . you might want to head in pretty quick." There was a pause. "We had an accident with a female ground crew member. She stepped into a snake hole when she was helping with a landing. Looks like her ankle is broken."

"Sorry to hear that. We're heading your way. We'll probably be there in another ten or fifteen minutes."

Alex waited politely until Tex put down the radio. "Some lady broke her ankle?"

"Yep. These fields aren't very smooth. She was probably looking up and not watching where she was stepping."

Alex leaned over the edge to see if he could still see the chase vehicle. Everything looked peaceful from way up high. It took him a minute to spot the Suburban again on a small road off to his right.

As they drifted closer to the high school, Alex noticed that the altimeter now read only sixty-nine hundred feet, and that the other gauge—he forgot what it was called—showed that they were still going down. All the other balloons were on the ground already, although some were still partly inflated.

Tex spoke into the radio. "Yellow Rose Chase, this is Yellow Rose. We're going to put down here in the field by the high school."

"Yellow Rose Chase. We're about a mile behind you, but we have you in sight. We'll be there."

Tex turned to Alex. "Remember what I told you about the variometer? If you watch the needle now, you'll see how fast we're going down."

Variometer, Alex thought. *That's what it was called.* The needle had dropped below the zero to the one hundred mark. "Right now we're going down one hundred feet per minute, right?" he asked.

"That's right. Boy, you learn quickly! Maybe you should be a pilot when you grow up."

"Maybe," Alex said. "I learn *some* things fast, but other times it's really hard for me. I have a learning disability called Attention Deficit Disorder. Sometimes it makes it hard at school."

"Really? Well, you sure picked up all this stuff fast."

Within a few minutes they were skimming only about three hundred feet above the empty fields. Now that they were closer to the ground, Alex was surprised to see how fast they were moving. They sped right over some of the other balloons on the ground. Alex leaned out and waved.

"Hmm," Tex said. He sounded worried. "The wind is pushing us right along that barbed wire fence below. I think we're going to have to try again somewhere else." Using the burner for a moment, he brought the balloon back up to six hundred feet.

They drifted over the thick wooded area next to the school, and then Tex let the Yellow Rose slowly drop again. As the altimeter sank from sixty-eight hundred to sixty-four hundred—only two hundred feet above the ground—Alex noticed that the field below was hilly and covered with snow. It gave him a funny feeling. They were still moving pretty fast. How hard would they slam into the ground?

Tex must have been thinking the same thing. "This is probably going to be a rough landing," he said. "I want you to squat down in the bottom of the basket now, and stay there. The wind is pushing us pretty hard, so we'll probably do a short drag in the snow."

Alex obediently dropped down onto the floor, wrapping his arms around his knees. He was just as glad not to have to watch the ground rush up to meet them. After another minute, Tex half-crouched down beside him.

"Here we go!" he said, bracing himself against the sides of the basket. "We're probably going to bump a few times." *Whoomp!*

The basket hit and then tipped over violently, toss-ing Alex onto his side. Scraping along the field like a snowplow, the basket scooped up wet snow, showering Alex with it. He sputtered and closed his eyes. Tex hadn't been kidding about a rough landing!

Then, just as suddenly, the wild bouncing stopped. Relieved, Alex opened his eyes and jumped up.

In that instant he realized two things: Tex was gone—and the Yellow Rose, with Alex inside, was once again rocketing skyward!

Back on the Ground

Minutes earlier, the crew in the chase vehicle had watched Tex's first landing attempt by the high school. The Yellow Rose dipped low and suddenly climbed back up. "Must have been some last-minute problem," Mr. Hollenbaugh told the Nicholoses. "Tex aborted his landing. Let's follow them on to the next field."

Stephanie, sitting next to her mom in the back, was happier than ever that she hadn't gone up in the balloon. Seeing her brother's tiny figure standing in that flimsy basket gave her goose bumps. What if it fell off? They'd drop like rocks!

Mr. Hollenbaugh followed the Yellow Rose past Black Forest, a thick patch of woods beside the school. Then, seeing that Tex was heading down over the large snowy field to their left, Mr. Hollenbaugh pulled over and parked. They all got out to watch the landing. "I'm sure Alex is so thrilled over all this," Mrs. Nicholos said with a smile. "He probably won't stop talking about it for weeks."

Mr. Nicholos laughed. "Yeah, he's a pretty fearless kid. This was a once-in-a-lifetime opportunity for him."

The Yellow Rose had already dropped down to one hundred feet. At the moment of landing, the dangling basket disappeared behind a small hump in the field. They could tell when it touched ground, though, by the movement of the balloon itself. It kind of tipped over and rippled sideways.

But before they could start across the field to meet Tex and Alex, the balloon shot back up into the sky.

"Wow! The wind must have caught Tex," said Mr. Hollenbaugh. "He had a really bad time with that landing."

They were turning to get back in the chase vehicle when Stephanie noticed a man scrambling over the snow hump, waving his arms frantically. "Hey look," she said, pointing. "There's a guy out there!"

As the man ran toward them, Stephanie thought how strange it was that he had been sitting all alone in the field. It must have scared him to have the big balloon land almost on his head. Maybe that was why they'd taken off again.

But Mr. Hollenbaugh was staring. "That looks like Tex!" he said in astonishment.

Stephanie stopped breathing. If that was Tex . . . where was Alex? With her stomach churning, she stared up at the Yellow Rose, already speeding away from them.

At that moment a panicked voice crackled over the radio in the van. "Help me!" it sobbed. "Help me, I'm scared!"

"That's *Alex!*" Stephanie cried.

Alone in the Sky

Alex's first thought, when he realized he was alone, was to jump. But when he leaned over the edge in a panic, he saw that the Yellow Rose was already hundreds of feet into the air. Far below, he could see Tex Houston scrambling to his feet in the snow.

"Oh, no!" Alex wailed. "Oh, *no!*" Frozen with fear, he gripped the edge of the basket. What should he do?

Then he remembered the radio. Fumbling his way over to it, he snatched up the microphone and pushed the button, the way he'd seen Tex do. "Help me!" he sobbed. "Help me, I'm scared!"

After a moment, a strong voice crackled back. "Alex, this is Dave. Are you OK? Are you OK?"

Relief washed over Alex at hearing the pilot's voice. "Yeah, I'm fine," he cried. "But I don't know what to do! I don't know how to fly this thing!"

"I'm going to help you. OK? Everything's going to be fine. Just calm down."

"OK."

Alex peered over the side again. He was right over a big bunch of trees . . . and they looked like they were getting closer! Heart pounding, he reached up and tugged the burner cord like he'd seen Tex do. The Yellow Rose shot up several hundred feet.

"Alex? Listen to me carefully. I don't want you to burn again unless I tell you. We don't want you to get too high, OK?"

"But I was getting close to the trees. I was afraid I was going to crash into them."

"I understand. You're doing fine. But listen, you're in charge now, so you're going to have to stay calm. You're not a passenger anymore; you're the pilot. I'm going to give you some flying lessons, right here over the radio, and then you're going to land the balloon. OK? Just do exactly what I tell you."

Alex nodded and then thought, *He can't see me nodding.* "OK," he said aloud. "I'm ready."

There was a long moment of silence. "All right," Mr. Hollenbaugh said. "First, I want you to look at the altimeter and tell me exactly what it says. That's a digital gauge with red numbers."

Alex said, "I know. Tex showed me which one it was. It reads 7-7-5-0."

"OK, that's fine. Now tell me what you see when you look straight ahead."

Still holding the radio mike in his hand, Alex looked forward. "Trees and hills and stuff," he said, "and a couple houses." He glanced behind him. "Where are you guys? I can't see you anymore."

"We're just a mile or two behind you. Don't worry, we can see you just fine."

Alex felt a sudden sickening sensation as the basket dropped away beneath his feet. "I'm falling!" he shouted. Panicked, he tugged at the burner cord, hard. The balloon rocketed skyward.

"Alex!" said Mr. Hollenbaugh. *"Don't use the burner unless I tell you. I won't let you crash, I promise."*

Alex's heart was still pounding. "I can't help it. It *feels* like I'm falling." He took a deep breath. "Can I talk to my mom for a minute?"

"Sure. Hang on." There was a pause, and then Mrs. Nicholos's voice said, "Hi, honey."

"Hi, Mom."

"You're doing great. I'm really proud of you."

Her voice sounded strange to Alex, but it was probably just the effects of radio. "Well, it's not like it's that hard," Alex said. "Tex taught me a lot. Is he OK? What happened to him?"

"He got dumped out when the basket went upside down. He chipped a tooth, but other than that he's fine. He's sitting right here. He says you're doing a great job." She paused. "Look, I'm going to turn you back over to Dave now. You just hang in there, OK?"

"OK. Bye, Mom."

"Alex?" It was Mr. Hollenbaugh's voice again. "I need you to look down and find another instrument for me. This one has a needle and a dial face. Do you see it?"

"That's called the very-something, right? Yeah, I see it. It's on zero, so I must be flying level."

"Good. OK, just keep an eye on the variometer and tell me if it dips down any. Then I'll tell you how long to burn."

Alex didn't want him to stop talking. "How long will it be before I can land?"

"Well, we just need to find a safe, level place without power lines or fences. You're flying over some rough country right now, so you just need to be patient. Tex says you have plenty of fuel, so you're OK."

Alex leaned his elbows on the edge of the basket, watching the trees far below. He noticed for the first time that the shadow of the balloon was dancing across the treetops.

"OK," he said in a small voice.

The Chase Is On

After Mrs. Nicholos handed the radio back over to Mr. Hollenbaugh, she pressed her fist against her mouth. She sobbed quietly, not wanting Alex to hear her. Stephanie was also crying. She scooted closer to her mother and buried her face in her coat.

Mr. Nicholos's face was gray with strain. "How much fuel does he actually have?" he asked Tex.

"We started out with enough fuel for two hours," Tex replied, "and the balloon's been up now for almost an hour. But Alex is light, so the fuel will last longer for him."

Tex was still dazed from the events of the last hour. When he first stumbled up to the chase vehicle, all he could say was, "I'm sorry, I'm sorry."

It had all happened so fast. The bump, the basket tilting upside down, him falling out into the snow . . . then his desperate grab for Alex. He'd had no time to pull the rip-line, the thick strap that opened the top of the balloon to let the hot air out. In less than three seconds the Yellow Rose had been airborne again.

The shaken pilot knew only too well the dangers of Alex's situation. If he used the burners too much, he could climb up out of radio range. He could run out of fuel. He could hit a power line, or catch the balloon on fire. He could panic and jump.

Dave Hollenbaugh spoke into the radio. "Alex, let's go ahead now and use the burner. But only for a second, OK? You ready?"

The boy's voice replied, "Ready."

"OK, only while I count. One . . . two . . . three . . . stop."

In the distance, the Yellow Rose glided upward and then leveled off. "Good," Mr. Hollenbaugh said. "That was perfect."

As soon as he let go of the mike, Mr. Hollenbaugh turned to speak to the Nicholoses. "I don't know the roads in the direction Alex is heading. Keep a lookout for a local person who can guide us."

They were passing a field when Mr. Nicholos spotted a rancher riding along on a tractor. "Stop!" he yelled. Jumping out, he ran over to tell the rancher what was happening. The man left his tractor and jumped into the car with them.

"I know these roads like the back of my hand," he said firmly. "Let's go!"

High overhead, Alex was finally starting to relax a little. Nothing really bad had happened yet, and he was getting pretty good at checking the instruments every few minutes. He only burned now when Mr. Hollenbaugh told him to. It was just like being a real pilot!

He peered out of the basket to watch the chase vehicle, driving along almost directly under him. Suddenly he grinned. The basket had scooped up a lot of snow. It would be funny to see if he could hit the Suburban with a snowball!

Squatting, he quickly molded a few snowballs into shape and then leaned out of the basket to take aim. "Bombs away!" he yelled, sending the first one flying. It sailed away through the air but landed in the field below, startling a small herd of cows. He didn't do much better with his second shot. He kept trying until all the snow was gone.

He was still pretty cheerful when Mr. Hollenbaugh told him it was time to burn again. But then Mr. Hollenbaugh said something that wiped the smile off his face.

"Listen, I've just been talking to Tex, and he thinks you should switch over to the other burner now.

You're probably starting to run low on fuel on the first tank."

Low on fuel? Alex didn't like the sound of that. "How much fuel *do* I have?"

"Tex says not to worry. You have plenty. We just want you to switch burners before you *have* to, so you don't have to do it in a hurry. OK?"

"OK."

"Tex says the second burner doesn't have a pullcord attached, so you're going to have to reach up higher to pull it. Can you see it?"

Heart pounding, Alex looked up. Sure enough, there was the second burner. He could just reach the lever by stretching all the way up on his tiptoes.

"I see it," he told the chase vehicle. "It's a good thing I'm tall, though, or I wouldn't be able to reach it." Without waiting for further instructions, he gave the lever a firm tug. Nothing happened.

He grabbed the mike. "Dave!" he screamed. "The burner won't go when I pull it! It's out of fuel! I'm gonna crash!"

Mr. Hollenbaugh's voice shot right back. It was strong and reassuring. "It's OK, Alex. You're not out of fuel; you just have to light the pilot light first. It's really easy . . . you just pull both burners at the same time."

Alex followed Mr. Hollenbaugh's instructions and then sighed with relief as flames roared up into the balloon again. "It worked," he reported.

Still Flying High

The incident left him a little shaken. What if he *did* end up running out of fuel? He'd just fall and fall . . . and crash. He was picturing what that would be like when he noticed a long rope coiled up on the floor of the basket.

He thought about tossing the rope over the side and sliding down it, but quickly gave up that idea. But maybe, if he threw it out, somebody on the ground could grab it and stop him!

He spoke into the mike. "Hey, Dave?" he said. "Can I throw out this long rope that's in here?"

There was a long moment of silence. "Go ahead," Mr. Hollenbaugh replied. "But be careful. Don't get tangled in it."

Alex grabbed an armful of rope and dropped it over the side. He watched as it snaked down, down, down. It ended a long way from the ground. Still, having it dangling there made him feel a little safer.

Mr. Hollenbaugh's voice crackled on the radio. "You know, Alex, that was a good idea. The rope is seventy-five feet long, and it makes it easier now for us to tell how far above the trees you are. We'll be coming out of the rough country here pretty soon, so we need to start watching for a place to land."

Alex peered ahead. "There's a big muddy field over the next clump of trees," he said. "It looks nice and soft. But there's a farmhouse in the middle of it. Can I still land there?"

There was a pause. "That sounds good. Now listen carefully. What's your altitude?"

Alex glanced at the altimeter. "It says 8205," he said.

"OK, that puts you about two thousand feet above the ground. We're going to bring you down now, nice and smooth, to about two hundred feet—that'll be 6400 on your altimeter—and then bring you the rest of the way down. We'll burn just enough to keep you dropping nice and slow. All right?"

"All right."

Even though the air was cold, Alex felt his palms getting sweaty. He didn't like the feeling as the Yellow Rose sank lower and lower over the trees. He could see the chase vehicle racing along the narrow road below, heading toward the same field. He was almost to the edge of the trees now. Suddenly the mud in the field ahead didn't look nearly as soft.

"What's your altimeter reading?" Mr. Hollenbaugh asked.

"I'm at 6420 feet," Alex replied. "But what about that farmhouse? It looks like I'm heading right for it. Should I burn again?"

"You've still got plenty of room. Burn to the count of three and then stop. We've got to keep you coming down."

It didn't look to Alex like he was that far from the ground, but he said doubtfully, "OK." The Yellow Rose glided down another one hundred feet.

"OK" Mr. Hollenbaugh said, "now listen to me carefully. You see the red strap hanging down from the top of the balloon? It should be tied to the edge of the basket."

Alex glanced around the basket till he spotted it. "Yeah, I see it."

"That's your rip-line. Don't pull it till I tell you to. It'll rip open a flap at the top of the balloon and let all the hot air out when you're landing."

"OK," Alex said. But when he glanced down he felt his throat tighten with fear. The ground seemed to be rushing up toward him. "I've got to burn again!" he said in a panic. "I'm falling too fast!" Without waiting for an answer he tugged the lever.

"Alex, *let go of that burner!*" Mr. Hollenbaugh's voice was sharp. "You're going to have to trust me on this. What's your altimeter reading now?"

Alex let go of the lever, breathing hard and deep. "It's 6360."

"All right. That's all right. Just stay with me now. You're up too high now to land this side of the house. We'll get you past the farmhouse and then you can land in one of the fields on the other side. Let's do another quick burn to give it plenty of room. It looks like there's a power line beside the house."

Alex tugged the lever carefully as Mr. Hollenbaugh counted. The Yellow Rose edged upward and glided over the farmhouse, the seventy-five-foot rope dangling barely forty feet from its roof.

"Perfect!" Mr. Hollenbaugh shouted. "Now just keep coming down. Looks like you're going to cross over the road right in front of us."

The Yellow Rose was now so low that Alex could almost make out faces inside the chase vehicle. He froze, his hand on the burner lever as he drifted across the narrow road. It felt like he was hurtling along at one hundred miles per hour!

"OK, Alex. Give one more quick burn to slow you down and then grab the rip-line and drop down in the basket. When I say, pull it as hard as you can."

Alex used the burner and then did as he was told. The moment he dropped down to the floor of the basket, Dave Hollenbaugh's voice shouted over the radio: "Pull! Pull! Pull!"

Alex hauled frantically at the line, trying not to picture the ground below. Seconds later, when something slammed hard against the basket, he didn't stop pulling. The basket tilted sideways and scraped—then stopped. He was on the ground.

From inside the chase vehicle, Stephanie watched with eyes wide as the balloon's basket touched ground and then skidded. The balloon then went limp and flat.

On Solid Turf

"He did it!" she screamed. "Alex did it!" Mr. and Mrs. Nicholos also screamed happily and then they all tumbled out of the Suburban to run across the field to Alex.

Inside the basket Alex was still pulling the red rip-line, not sure yet whether he was really down. When his family ran up, laughing and crying, he crawled out of the basket and stood up. He still felt a little dazed.

Stephanie flung herself at him, hugging him around the waist. Mr. Nicholos swooped him up in his arms and hugged him so hard Alex thought he would choke. Mrs. Nicholos, tears running down her cheeks, threw her arms around all of them.

"You're OK!" she sobbed. "Oh, thank God!"

Alex smiled shakily. "Gee, I'm sorry I got you guys all upset. I didn't mean to."

Mrs. Nicholos dried her tears. "We know that," she said, half laughing and half crying. "We're just glad you're all right!"

After a few minutes Alex went over to the Suburban where he met Dave Hollenbaugh for the first time. Mr. Hollenbaugh, who had been so calm and clear-headed throughout Alex's thirty-five-mile flight, was sitting there crying.

Alex stared, surprised to see that his radio friend had gray hair. "Gee," he blurted out, "you sounded a lot younger over the radio."

Mr. Hollenbaugh chuckled, wiping his eyes. "Believe me, Alex, before this happened, I was!" Everybody laughed.

"Well," Alex said, "you really gave good directions. I don't think I could've done it if you hadn't kept talking to me. Thanks a lot."

Mr. Hollenbaugh patted him on the back. "You were a good student. Or I should say," he added, "a good *pilot!*"

Tex had been listening quietly, but now he stepped forward. "I have something for you," he said seriously. "I think you earned these today." Carefully unpinning the silver pilot's wings from his chest, he pinned them to Alex's shirt. Everybody clapped and cheered.

Alex stared at the wings, his face splitting in a huge grin. "Thanks!" he said. "I guess now that I've done this, I can probably do just about anything, huh?"

Mrs. Nicholos leaned down to kiss him right in front of everybody. "Maybe not *anything,*" she said, laughing as his face turned beet red. "I'll believe that when I see you put my toaster back together again!"

Alex Nicholos (left) with Dave Hollenbaugh, the pilot who talked him down when the Yellow Rose took off.

Daniel and Serét at Calvary Christian Academy

Rescue in the Trinity River

The Serét Gomez & Daniel Whitehead Story

"C'mon, Barry, hurry up! We're gonna be late!" Daniel Whitehead, a muscular sixteen-year-old stood at the bottom of the stairs jingling his car keys impatiently. When his twelve-year-old brother finally clomped downstairs, yawning, Daniel pushed him outside. They had almost an hour's drive ahead to get to school in Fort Worth, Texas.

It was a chilly February day, and the sky was gray and cloudy. They both hurried over to the beige Oldsmobile in the driveway. Daniel jumped in and slipped his key into the ignition, but before he could close the door a metallic male voice boomed:

"YOUR KEY IS IN THE IGNITION. YOUR KEY IS IN THE IGNITION. YOUR KEY IS IN TH—"

Daniel slammed his door irritably, shutting off the computer-nagging. "I *know* my key is in the ignition!" he snapped. "I *put* it in the ignition!" He loved the car, but the computer-voice didn't always make sense. Did everybody but him always close their car door before putting in the key?

Barry, next to him, grinned at the outburst, and then settled back and closed his eyes. He hated getting up at 5:30 in the morning. By the time they pulled out of the driveway he was drifting back to sleep.

Soon they were driving smoothly down the high-way, Daniel humming softly to the radio. He liked music, just about all kinds. He played piano for his church youth group and sometimes wrote his own songs. He hoped to cut a record someday.

His little brother snoozed right up until they were pulling into the school parking lot. Then he stretched and sat up, yawning. "Are we there?" he asked sleep-ily, smacking his dry lips.

"Yeah, we're here," Daniel said. "You better sit up and straighten your shirt. You're all wrinkly."

"I don't care. I hate these stupid uniforms. I look like a dork."

Daniel grinned. "Well, little brother, I hate to break this to you, but you *are* a dork." He reached over to ruffle Barry's hair affectionately. "But don't worry about it. One day, if you're lucky, you might grow out of dorkhood."

"Yeah, right," Barry said. "Well, at least I don't talk to the car like you do. You act like there's a little invisible car guy hiding under the seat who pops out to say, 'Your key is in the ignition!'"

They were still trading brotherly insults as they walked up the steep parking lot toward the school. Calvary Christian Academy sat on top of a small hill, A large white building attached to a church, it over-looked Forest Park Boulevard, a busy four-lane high-way running along the banks of the Trinity River. Students who drove to school had to park in the lowest parking lot. The teachers thought it was good exercise for them to climb the hill every day.

"Hey, Brandon!" Daniel called, spotting a friend from drama class. Tall and skinny, Brandon had a leading role in the new school play with Daniel. He was known throughout the school for his witty "im-prov" performances, where he had to make up his lines as he went along. He was always surrounded by a crowd, and they were usually laughing.

"Hey, Farris!" Brandon called back. "What're you doing?"

In his first year at the private school, Daniel decided to change his image. Tired of being plain old Daniel, he had introduced himself by his middle name, Farris. He'd thought it sounded kind of bold and different, out of the ordinary. His Farris days hadn't lasted long, but the name had stuck with a few close friends.

"You seen Serét?" Daniel asked. Serét—pronounced "Sur-ray"—Gomez was a pretty senior with dark hair and eyes. She was also in drama class and the director of their current play, *Catacombs*. She and Brandon were always clowning around together.

"I haven't seen her this morning yet, but I bet she's around here somewhere." Brandon laughed. "She's probably running around in her socks, like usual. You know her!"

Daniel grinned. Serét was always getting in trouble for ditching her shoes, but no amount of scolding seemed to reform her. She just smiled brightly and kept "accidentally" leaving them at her desk, or in the gym, or in the choir room. Daniel liked her cheerful personality, not to mention her looks. It was too bad she was two whole years ahead of him in school.

A few minutes later he passed Serét in the hall, but he didn't really get to talk to her until computer class. They were computer partners.

"Hiya, Farris," she greeted him when he walked into class. She was wearing her usual green plaid jumper, white blouse, and—no shoes. Daniel stifled a smile.

"Hi," he said, sitting down and rolling his chair over next to hers. "Hey, gr-r-reat outfit!"

Serét punched him on the arm. "I keep dreaming of the day I graduate, when I can burn this awful uniform. Ahhh, what a thought! Too bad you'll have to wait two whole years, you poor little sophomore. Ha!"

Quick as lightning, Daniel braced his foot against the bottom of her chair and gave it a shove, sending her rolling backwards across the floor. Unfortunately, the computer teacher picked that very moment to walk in.

"What's going on here?" she demanded as Serét whizzed past, laughing, unable in her slippery socks to stop the chair. It bumped against a desk and stopped with a jolt. Serét quickly straightened her skirt and smiled up at the teacher.

"Oh, hi!" she said innocently. "My chair just kind of, um, moved. I'll put it back."

She hastily scooted back over to Daniel, waiting until the teacher looked away to hiss: "OK, Farris, you just wait till play rehearsal today. Payback time!"

"Do your worst," he whispered back with a grin. "It was worth it to watch your little *senior* face as you went flying across the room."

Serét's dark eyes sparkled. She enjoyed the playful battles she got into with Daniel. They fought over the computer keyboard, argued about where to sit at lunch, and teased each other constantly. He was a lot of fun and good-looking in a kind of goofy way. He had always been like a brother to her . . . although sometimes she wished he'd look at her less like a sister and more like a girl!

I should be ashamed of myself, Serét thought. *I've already got a boyfriend.* But lately, she had been thinking a lot more about Daniel than about him. Maybe it was time to move on.

Drama and Challenge

She was still mulling the idea when she got to drama class that afternoon. But when she spotted Daniel across the room, her romantic ideas were suddenly replaced with mischief. She called Brandon aside. "I've decided to give Farris a little acting exercise today," she confided. "A kind of challenge, you know?"

Brandon grinned down at her from his six-foot height. He and Serét both had reputations as wild joke-players. They often confused new students at school by pretending to be brother and sister.

"What are you going to do?" he asked.

Serét smiled. "*Good* actors can keep their focus no matter what's going on around them, right?"

"Absolutely."

"Well, I'm just going to give Farris a chance to prove how good he is. Tell everybody I want them to torture him while he's supposed to be unconscious. Once he wakes up I'm going to get in his face. I bet he'll get so nervous he'll forget all his lines."

Brandon chuckled. "I bet you're right. You're a cold woman, Serét."

"I try, I try," she said smugly.

Serét ducked into the bathroom to change into sweatpants and a T-shirt before starting the rehearsal. Since she often ended up climbing around on chairs or crawling on the floor, her green-plaid jumper wasn't a good idea.

The drama teacher took her seat at the back of the room as Serét made all the actors take their places. She was a good actress as well as a director, and she had a real talent for getting the students to play their roles.

Daniel was stretched out flat on the floor, supposedly unconscious. He'd worn his glasses that day instead of his contacts, so he took them off and put them in his pocket. He was supposed to be a mysterious stranger who'd just been dragged in, nearly dead, from the cold. His rescuers were a small group of starving fugitives on the run from an evil government.

As the scene opened, one of the fugitives leaned over him anxiously. "He looks dead," she said loudly and then added in a low voice, "Let's eat him."

Daniel's lips twitched, but he didn't smile. Another girl brought a blanket to cover him. "Do you think he's a spy?" she asked, adding softly, "Let's cook him first."

By then Daniel was having to hold his breath to keep from laughing. Serét walked up to the group. "Keep going!" she called. "Ignore me and stay in your parts!"

The "rescuers" continued to talk back and forth, always adding whispered comments like, "Mmm, I'm hungry."

Serét slipped in among them and nudged Daniel hard with her foot. Startled, he half-opened one eye to see who was kicking him, forgetting he'd taken his glasses off. Serét was just a dark-haired blur.

"You're unconscious!" she told him sternly. "Don't you move, no matter what I do!" When Daniel closed his eye again, she grinned wickedly at Brandon.

Finally Daniel "woke up" and looked around in a daze. The girls gave him coffee to revive him, and then the leader of the fugitives approached. "Who are you?" he asked suspiciously. "What's your name?"

"James Smith," Daniel mumbled.

That was Brandon's cue. He stalked over and glared down at Daniel. "Sounds fake," he snapped. "Who are your parents, John and Pocahontas?"

Serét slipped in front of Brandon before Daniel could answer, deliberately blocking his view of Brandon. "Stay focused," she told Daniel sweetly. "Pretend I'm not here."

"Actually, I'm the second son of John and Beverly," Daniel said to Serét's knees. "Next question?" The rehearsal ended in a burst of laughter. Daniel jumped up to chase Serét around the set and then walked with her out to her car.

"Next time you mess with me like that, I'm going to make you sorry," he said. "That was bad!"

"I told you I'd pay you back for rolling me across the room. And right in front of the teacher! I get in enough trouble on my own, you know."

"Got that right. Well, I need to go find my little brother. I guess I'll see you tomorrow."

Serét flashed him a bright smile. "Yep."

Just then Barry ran up, his shirttail hanging out in back. Daniel waved to Serét and then started toward his car, humming to himself. He got in, slipped in the key, then jumped as a familiar metallic voice boomed: "YOUR KEY IS IN THE IGNITION . . . YOUR KEY IS—"

Barry snickered as Daniel slammed his hand against the steering wheel and then shut his door. The invisible car guy had gotten him again. Daniel was shaking his head. "One of these days I'm going to figure out how to disconnect that thing . . . maybe send it to car heaven with a set of slashed wires. Serve it right for being so stupid."

On the way home, Daniel's thoughts kept drifting back to Serét. He'd always liked her cheerful attitude and how she lived life to the fullest. It might be fun to take her out sometime . . . if, that is, he got to date sometime before he was thirty!

The trouble was, he was probably the only sixteen-year-old guy in America who wasn't allowed to date yet. That was one of the problems with having a dad who was a preacher. His parents had made up this weird rule: before any of the kids in their family could start dating, they had to read the entire Bible aloud, cover to cover, no skipping. Not only that, but they couldn't start reading until their fifteenth birthdays. Daniel's two big sisters, now married and gone, had managed it in less than a year, but he hadn't been quite as motivated. Now he wished he'd put in a little more effort.

He and Barry didn't get home until about five o'clock. When they opened the front door, two small torpedo-shaped dachshunds launched themselves happily at their knees. Barry leaned down to pet them, but Daniel just rolled his eyes and stepped over them. Precious and Sugarbaby were his mother's yappy, clothes-chewing, irritating little doglets. He wouldn't have minded having a *real* dog—a German shepherd, or maybe a rottweiler—but his mom wouldn't hear of it. She was probably afraid her wimpy little dogs would get eaten for breakfast. Daniel grinned, enjoying the thought.

He strolled into the kitchen, hoping this might be one of the rare times there'd actually be some food in the house. His mom was a great cook, but she only made real meals once in awhile. The problem was, none of them were ever home at the same time. They all just grabbed food and ran.

He opened the refrigerator and peered hopefully inside and then sighed. As usual, the shelves were bare. Even the leftover sauerkraut and wienies from earlier that week were gone. He pulled a box of dry macaroni and cheese out of the pantry, shook it a few times, and then put it back. He had to be at church for youth group by 6:30, so there wasn't time to cook anything.

"Looks like peanut butter and jelly again," he told Barry. "Mom might be bringing stuff home with her, though. She should be here in a few minutes."

Barry wrinkled his nose. "I'll wait," he said. "I had peanut butter for lunch."

Daniel slapped a sandwich together and ran upstairs to change clothes, taking two steps at a time. Between school, drama, track team, and church, he stayed pretty busy, even without dating. Still . . . maybe next week, if things slowed down, he'd get around to some serious Bible reading. It would be worth it if he finally got to take Serét out, not that it wasn't worth it for its own sake.

Serét was, at that same moment, talking about Daniel. "It was so funny in drama class, Dad," she said. She and Mr. Gomez were on their way home after running some after-school errands. "I told the whole cast to give Farris a hard time. They all kept whispering about cutting him up and cooking him for dinner while he was supposed to be unconscious. It was great!"

Mr. Gomez grinned. "Pretty good, Tiger. I wish I could've been there to watch."

Serét flinched at the nickname. It had started years before, when Disney's *Jungle Book* cartoon had first come out. Her dad jokingly called her "Tiger," and the name stuck. Later, Serét wondered why she'd been nicknamed after the movie's bad guy, the smooth-talking Sheer Kahn, instead of one of the nicer animals. She didn't remember being *that* bad as a little kid!

Besides, unlike most of her friends—Farris, for instance—she actually liked her real name. Serét had a romantic ring to it. Her parents had named her after a beautiful French actress they read about in a magazine. At any rate, it sounded a lot better than Tiger!

When they got home, Mrs. Gomez was waiting. Like Serét, she had thick, dark hair and dark eyes. Her grandparents were from Spain.

"Hi, you two!" Mrs. Gomez said as they breezed in. "How was work and school?"

"Work was fine," Mr. Gomez replied. He was a commercial artist who drew pictures for labels and signs. Mrs. Gomez was an accountant.

"School was OK," Serét said. "But I'd rather talk about food. What's for dinner?"

In their house, Mr Gomez was the main cook. "Well, let's see," he said. "How about some spaghetti?"

"Works for me," Serét said. "Let's get moving. I'm starving!"

The small kitchen got pretty crowded with all three of them trying to help. While Mr. Gomez searched the refrigerator for an onion, Serét tracked down a box of noodles. Mrs. Gomez watched from a safe distance, sitting at the kitchen table.

"So," Mr. Gomez said, "how was your day at work?"

Mrs. Gomez sighed. "Oh, OK mostly. But I had this one client who was a real jerk. He argued with everything I said."

Mr. Gomez straightened, an onion in hand. "That's too bad. I thought you looked kind of tired."

Serét hated it when her parents started griping about work. It was one of the few times she wished she had a brother or sister around to talk to. Gloomy parents were no fun at all.

She cleared her throat, hoping to distract them. "I say we hang him," she said seriously. "Death to all jerk clients!" She emphasized her point by waving the dry noodles in the air.

Both her parents laughed. "If only it was that easy," Mrs. Gomez said. But at least now she was smiling about it.

Mr. Gomez was standing at the counter, starting to chop the onion. When Serét bent down to pull a pot from the cabinet, she banged the cabinet door against his shin.

"Ouch!" he yelped, hopping on one foot. "What are you trying to do, cripple me?"

"Uh-huh," Serét agreed, smiling sweetly. "I always wanted a one-legged father. I think that would be cool. Don't you, Mom?"

"Oh, no, you two leave me out of this," Mrs. Gomez said. "I'm not getting in the middle of one of your silly battles. I know better."

Serét and Mr. Gomez teased back and forth as they cooked hamburger, stirred sauce, and boiled noodles. Mr. Gomez "accidentally" dropped a piece of onion down Serét's back, and Serét "accidentally" banged his head with the refrigerator door. But finally, it looked like everything was ready.

"I get to test the noodles!" Serét said. Using a fork, she fished out one spaghetti strand, and with a dramatic gesture threw it against the kitchen wall. The rule was, if noodles stuck to the wall, they were done; if they slid off, they needed to be cooked a little longer. This time, the noodle stuck.

"Perfect!" Mr. Gomez said. Before Serét could stop him, he snatched the noodle off the wall and dropped it on top of her head. It dangled down onto her face like a long white worm.

"Dad!" she shrieked. Laughing, Mr. Gomez ducked around the corner into the living room.

That night they decided to eat in front of the TV. Serét liked to watch TV shows and pick out the things the actors were doing wrong. Like her French namesake, she dreamed of becoming a great actress.

"Just look at that girl!" she exclaimed in disgust, pointing with a forkful of spaghetti. "She doesn't even know her lines, and she keeps turning her back to the camera. Where'd they find her, anyway? Actors-R-Us?"

"Now, now, Tiger," her father said. "You'll get your chance someday."

"Sure, years from now," Serét grumped. "I just wish I didn't have to wait so long. Drama class is fun, but I wish something dramatic would happen in real life. Maybe I should rob a bank or something."

"Great idea!" Mr. Gomez said. "We could split the profits." He dropped his voice and added in a loud whisper: "We just have to make sure your mother doesn't find out. She would probably turn us in!"

Mrs. Gomez smiled. "I certainly would! I swear, both of you should be actors, the way you carry on!"

Mr. Gomez puffed his chest out proudly. "The woman recognizes great acting talent when she sees it, eh, Tiger?"

"Absolutely. Now, let's talk about the bank robbery . . . "

Another Normal Day?

The next morning, when Daniel and Barry walked in through the school's front double doors, Serét was waiting. She fell into step beside Daniel as he started down the hall.

"Hey, Farris, ready for play rehearsal this afternoon?" she asked innocently.

"I don't know," Daniel said, raising an eyebrow. "What are you planning today? Set me on fire?"

"Hmm, now that's an interesting thought. Hadn't planned on it, but I'll keep it in mind for next time." Laughing and talking, they strolled down the hall together until they reached their first-period classes.

At noon, Serét talked Daniel, Brandon, and several other friends into skipping lunch—not hard, considering the menu. They all went back to the music room to sit around and talk.

Brandon stretched out across four chairs, putting his hands behind his head. "You know, Serét, I was thinking the other day about back when we were in eighth grade," he said. "Remember how bad everybody treated us?"

Serét nodded. "I think we were the two ugly ducklings of the school. I was kind of short and pudgy, and you were a skinny little geek. Nobody wanted to hang around with us." She laughed. "That's probably why we bonded. We were the only ones who'd talk to us."

"Yeah." Brandon grinned. "But just look at us now. We're the two most popular people on the face of the planet!"

Daniel groaned. "I think I'm going to be sick!" Brandon and Serét both laughed.

After lunch, the rest of the school day passed quickly. When the last-period bell rang, Daniel gathered his books and headed for drama class. Time for him to be transformed once again into James Smith, Mysterious Stranger.

This time, Serét kept the rehearsal serious. "OK, people, let's start where Captain Slater is asking Smith to betray his friends."

Daniel took his place among the ragged band of "fugitives." Slater stalked up to him, frowning.

"You're no use to me dead, Smith," he snapped. "What's your decision?"

Daniel hesitated—then, without warning, leaped for Slater's throat. He fought like a tiger as the other officers grabbed him by the arms. They slammed him against the wall, tied him to a chair, and then hit him in the face.

Serét stepped between them, clapping her hands. "That's better!" she said. "But let's go over that again and work on the hitting part. It still looks a little fake."

Daniel rubbed his neck. "It feels pretty real to me," he complained. "That wall isn't exactly soft, you know."

Serét shook her head sadly. "I guess you're just not cut out to be a hero, Farris. Here, let me show you how it's done."

She walked over to take his place in front of the fugitive group. "OK, let's take it from the top of this scene!"

Everything was fine until they reached the part where Smith was slammed into the wall. The police, used to Daniel's bigger size and weight, almost slammed Serét through the wall. Dizzy, she sank down onto the chair, holding her head.

"Gee, you guys," she said. "Why not just kill me next time? You almost knocked me out!"

Daniel patted her shoulder. "Are you all right?"

"I think so. But from now on you do your own stunts. I guess I'm not cut out to be a hero either."

They were still working on the scene when the 3:30 bell rang. As everyone stampeded for the door, Serét jumped up on a chair to yell: "Remember to work on memorizing your parts! Next week we're rehearsing without scripts!"

"Slave driver," Brandon said cheerfully as he walked past. He wiggled the chair she was standing on, causing her to shriek and jump down. "Don't you know you're too short to scare anybody?" he added.

Serét shot back, "Don't you know you could be replaced with a first-grader? In fact, a first-grader could probably even act better." They parted with those friendly words.

Daniel stayed behind after the others left. Barry had a basketball game after school, so there was no hurry for him to get home. Besides, Serét was good company.

"So, what are you up to this afternoon?" Serét asked as she put on her jacket and found her purse.

Daniel slipped on his own gray bomber jacket and grabbed his books. "Just hanging around until my brother's game is over. Then I'll probably go home and wash my car. It's filthy." He laughed. "Exciting life, huh?"

"Oh, I don't know," said Serét. "When me and my cousin were younger, we'd always wash the car in our bathing suits so we could slide down the windshield and stuff. It was a lot of fun."

Daniel followed her out into the noisy hall, grinning. "Well, next time you and your cousin are washing a car, why don't you call me over so I can watch? Sounds like it might be kind of entertaining."

Serét rolled her eyes. "Give it up, Farris." Stepping out into the chilly air, she pulled her jacket closer. "Brr, it's cold today. You wouldn't catch me in a swimsuit in this weather!"

"Too bad," Daniel joked.

Still chatting, they walked down the slope to the lower parking lot. Daniel wanted to throw his books in his car, so Serét waited as he pulled out his keys.

He had just turned the key in the lock when a terrified scream ripped the air. Startled, they both whirled around.

Near the entrance of the school, a woman dressed in jeans, a denim jacket, and a small blue hat stood frozen, staring down at the grassy slope that divided the upper and lower parking areas. As Daniel and Serét watched, the woman screamed again and then began running down the slope, waving her arms. Her hat blew off and tumbled across the grass, but she didn't stop.

"What—?" Serét said, but Daniel cut her off.

"Look!" he said, pointing. A station wagon was rolling down the slope below the woman—out of control and quickly gaining speed. "That must be her car! Come on!"

Dropping their books, both teenagers took off running. They veered off to their right, trying to intersect the runaway car. It shot into the parking area below them, heading straight for a telephone pole at the bottom.

"Dear God, my kids!" the woman screamed. "My kids!"

Countdown to Terror

Her words sent chills down Daniel's and Serét's spines. Feet pounding the pavement, they ran even faster. By now the car was going almost twenty miles per hour. Daniel threw off his jacket and then used all his track team skill to pull ahead of Serét.

Despite all his efforts, though, Daniel was still too far away to do anything when the car reached the telephone pole. At the last moment, as if by its own choice, the station wagon somehow veered, missing the thick pole by inches.

Daniel sighed with relief, but only for a moment. The runaway car was now hurtling straight for the busy four-lane highway!

The sobbing woman, running down from the opposite direction, was now almost even with Daniel. He shouted over to her breathlessly: "Are your kids in the car?"

"Yes!" she cried. "Please save my babies!"

Daniel nodded. If the station wagon was empty, he might have hesitated before chasing it out onto the highway. But there was no way he was going to stand back and let innocent little kids get hurt!

The car's front wheels were now just feet from the pavement. Still more than thirty feet behind, Daniel saw a little girl trying to scramble over into the back, and what looked like another small head bobbing around the back seat. Just ahead, the heavy afternoon traffic whizzed by in both directions on the highway.

Daniel yelled and waved his arms, trying to alert the other drivers. Behind him, he heard the mother's terrified scream as the car carrying her children burst out into traffic. After only a brief pause at the curb, Daniel dashed out onto the highway after it.

His heart pounded wildly as horns blared and tires screeched on every side. But he didn't look around, even when air brakes hissed and an eighteen-wheeler truck skidded to a stop just feet from his body. He sprinted on, not noticing that the bearded truck driver and several other people had jumped out of their cars to join the chase.

The station wagon somehow made it safely across the highway. But a much worse danger lay just ahead—the wide, deep waters of the Trinity River.

The steep bank was less than twenty feet from the pavement. Even as Daniel gained on the car, he realized with despair that he'd never be able to stop it in time. He only had seconds to catch up, jerk open the driver's door, jump in, and hit the brakes.

It was impossible.

You've got to help me out here, God, he prayed in despair. *Those kids are in trouble.*

Beside the highway was stretched a thin steel cable, kind of like a guard rail. For a moment Daniel hoped it might stop the runaway car, but the heavy station wagon snapped it like a piece of thread. Bumping over the grass and gravel, it hurtled down the steep river-bank toward the water.

"No!" Daniel screamed. Still running, he watched in horror as the car shot off the bank. It seemed to hang in the air for a moment and then tilted to splash nose-first into the deep, fast-moving water. "*No!*"

The hysterical mother rushed up behind him with Serét. "My babies are in there!" she shrieked. The car, barely afloat, was already being swept downstream. "Dear God, I can't swim! *I can't swim!*"

Daniel acted instantly. Sprinting to the edge of the riverbank, he dived in after the car. The cold made him gasp, and his clothes and shoes dragged him down. His glasses were also ripped off, but he didn't stop to grab for them. He had to get the kids out before the car sank!

Swimming hard, he reached the back of the station wagon and then pulled himself around to the front passenger door. He grabbed the door handle and tugged hard, but it wouldn't budge.

Helpless, he looked inside. A baby girl was staring up at him from her infant seat; she had wide eyes and a frilly white headband around her head. Two other children, a girl about five and a boy about three, were in the backseat, screaming and beating against the glass. Daniel looked around wildly. There *had* to be some way to get them out!

Help to the Rescue

Suddenly, a small bearded man appeared in the water beside him. It was the driver of the eighteen-wheeler. "The back window's open a little!" he shouted. "Let's try to break it out!"

Daniel nodded. The car was already dipping lower in the water. They didn't have much time. Swimming to the back window, they both curled their fingers over the top of the glass and then jerked as hard they could. On their second try, the window broke off in their hands.

The truck driver let the glass sink and then moved forward to attack the front door again. Daniel reached in the back window and grabbed the little girl. She was wearing a plaid dress and had her hair in braids.

"Come on!" he said. "You've got to get out of there!"

She climbed out, sobbing, and wrapped her arms around his neck. Behind her, her little brother was also wailing. Daniel hesitated, wanting to take him, too. But the current was too strong. If he tried to take both children they might all drown.

Turning to kick off from the car, he almost ran into Serét. She was treading water right behind him, her dark eyes wide.

"Get the boy!" he sputtered. "The car's starting to sink!"

"OK!" she said.

As Daniel started away from the car, the little girl clung to him, almost choking him. He wanted to calm her down by talking to her, but it was a struggle to even keep his face above water. His shoes felt like lead weights. He began to wonder if he was strong enough to make it all the way back to shore. The current kept shoving him back toward the car.

Behind him, Serét was also having trouble. The terrified little boy wouldn't come to her. Somehow, she had to get him to the window!

"It's OK," she told him, hanging on to the side of the car. "I'll take you to your mommy." Slowly, fearfully, the boy crept closer. She grabbed him and pulled him out into the water, surprised at how heavy he felt.

The truck driver had tried both front doors without success. The water was now covering the car's hood, and was almost up to the open window. His beard dripping, his thin hair plastered to his head, the man swam back to Serét.

"I've got to get that baby out!" he said. "The car's going to sink any second. I'm going to try to climb in through the back!"

Holding the boy with one arm, Serét splashed away from the window to make room for him. The minute she let go of the car, though, she sank up to her nose. Panicking, she kicked as hard as she could. No matter what happened to her, she had to keep the boy's face above water. She *had* to! On shore somewhere off to her left, somebody yelled something. Serét couldn't make out the words. Heart pounding, she clawed her way across the water, trying to block out everything but swimming. Every stroke was a struggle, and it grew harder and harder to catch even a gasp of air. Her lungs felt like they were going to explode.

She was still a long way from shore when she realized with despair that she might not make it. She was choking on water, moving in slow motion. The current was too strong for her. Her arms and legs felt like lead.

With the last of her strength she pushed the little boy higher, silently screaming: *I need help!*

Daniel and the little girl had just reached shore. A small crowd was gathered on the bank, and several people helped them up. Exhausted, Daniel handed the child to her mother and then collapsed on the grass.

"Faith!" the woman sobbed, peeling off her jacket to wrap it around the little girl. "Faithie! Oh, God, thank you. Thank you!"

Daniel took several huge gulps of air, glad to be able to breathe again. The cold wind hitting his wet clothes left him numb and shivering. He wished he had the energy to go find his jacket.

After a moment, though, he remembered Serét. When he sat up and looked out over the water, his heart leaped into his throat. Serét was about halfway between the car and shore, splashing weakly, her dark head barely above water. The little boy in her arms was scared and crying. It looked like they were drowning!

Fear in the River

Before he could scramble to his feet, however, a big man wearing jeans and a T-shirt charged up beside him and dived off the bank into the icy water. He swam straight for Serét.

Reaching her side, the man snatched the little boy from Serét's arms. With the child's weight gone, the petite teen was able to struggle back to the surface and catch her breath. When the big man started back toward shore carrying the boy, she swam after him.

Relieved, Daniel glanced back out at the car. Water was flooding through the broken window, making the car tilt forward. The small truck driver had wriggled his way inside. He was in the front, frantically jerking at the infant seat.

"Hurry!" the mother screamed. "Please hurry!"

Daniel stood up just as a slender blond-haired man raced over from the highway and dived in. With strong, sure strokes, he swam with the current out toward the car.

Serét and the man carrying the little boy reached shore and were greeted by the crowd. The big man—his name turned out to be Allan McGinnis—looked almost sick; he had to be helped the last few feet. One of the other bystanders carried the boy up to his mother and sister.

"Oh, Stephen!" the woman cried, taking him into her arms. The sobbing three-year-old popped his thumb in his mouth and snuggled his head into her shoulder.

Daniel ran down the bank to help Serét. Her hands were shaking.

"You OK?" he asked.

"Yeah," she said, pushing her wet hair back from her face. "I just need to sit for a minute. My legs are wobbly."

They sat together on the windy bank and looked out across the water. The blond-haired man was now almost to the car. Just as he swam up, the man inside got the baby unstrapped from her car seat. He snatched her up and crawled over into the backseat, fighting the water gushing in through the broken window. He shoved the squirming baby out into the other man's arms.

The car suddenly shifted, nosing deeper into the water. Serét shrieked. "Get out!" she yelled in a panic. "Hurry, it's sinking!"

She and Daniel both watched helplessly, horror stricken at the thought of what would happen if the car sank with the man trapped inside. *Please let him get out in time,* Serét prayed. *Please . . .*

Slinging the baby up over one shoulder, the blond-haired man quickly splashed away from the car. The man inside dived for the window. Wriggling his way out, he kicked off from the side of the car just as it shifted one last time—then sank with a swirl!

"He made it!" Serét yelled, jumping up and down and pounding on Daniel's arm.

"He's out!"

Sirens were wailing in the distance by the time the other man reached shore with the baby. Scrambling up the bank, he quickly placed her in her mother's arms.

"Thank you!" the woman said tearfully. "Thank you so much!" She cradled the baby close, trying to shield her from the wind. The infant's only injury was a tiny cut on her head.

The blond-haired man said his name was Rodger Brownlee. "I didn't do much," he said, shaking water from his shoes. "That guy with the beard is the one who got her out of the car."

The bearded man was just climbing up the bank. As he passed Daniel and Serét, they saw with astonishment that he was wearing heavy cowboy boots. How on earth had he managed to swim in those?

"Is the baby OK?" he asked the crowd, wringing out his shirt sleeves.

The people gathered around the mother and baby parted as an ambulance pulled off the highway into the grass, its lights flashing. A police car pulled up at the same time. Several paramedics jumped out.

"I think she's fine," Serét said. "I think they're all OK."

The bearded truck driver, whose name turned out to be Skip Womack, nodded. "That's good. I have kids of my own. I couldn't just sit there and let them sink like that."

"Us either," Daniel said.

Before climbing into the ambulance, the grateful mother ran over to hug Daniel, Serét, and the three other rescuers. She introduced herself as Joy Warren.

"I just stuck my head inside to yell for my two oldest kids," she explained, "and when I turned around, I saw the car rolling down the hill! I'd turned it off and taken the keys, but one of the kids must've bumped the gearshift into neutral."

She shook her head, tears streaming down her cheeks. "I don't know what to say. You people are all heroes!"

Daniel and Serét waved as the ambulance pulled away. The crowd slowly cleared as people got back into their cars and drove away. Together, the two teenagers started the long walk back to the school.

"Heroes," Serét said aloud. "Hey, Farris, what do think about that?"

Daniel shrugged. His lips and fingernails were almost blue from the cold water. "I don't think there was anything very heroic about what we did," he said.

"It wasn't like we had time to think about it or anything. It happened so fast."

"Yeah" . . . Serét sighed. "Still, it was pretty exciting. I've always kind of wished something dramatic would happen. I was telling my dad the other day that I might have to rob a bank just to liven things up."

Daniel laughed. "Knowing you, you might just get away with it! Was this enough excitement for you?"

"Definitely," Serét said, "I think after this I'll be perfectly happy keeping all the drama on stage." She shivered. "I'm freezing. I'm going to change back into my dry uniform."

"Me too." Daniel looked at her and then grinned. "On second thought," he said, "since you're already wet and everything, you could always help me wash my car. I hear it's a lot of fun to slide down the windshield."

"Farris!" Serét said, laughing. She chased him, her shoes squishing with each step, back up through the parking lot.

Brandon Abston enjoys a family cookout.

Apartment Inferno!

The Brandon Abston Story

"And the winner is—Misti!"

Grandpa Willard, tall and chubby with a shiny bald spot and glasses, held up a colorful crayon picture of a scarecrow and then handed eight-year-old Misti her prize: two crisp one-dollar bills.

"Thanks, Grandpa!" she said happily. "Look everybody!"

Brandon, twelve, grinned as he watched his young cousin dance back across the room, waving her prize money over her head. The coloring contest was part of his family's Thanksgiving tradition in Lawton, Oklahoma, but he knew Grandpa Willard wouldn't stop having contests until everybody won. It was his way of keeping the kids out of trouble while their mothers and aunts cooked a big Thanksgiving dinner.

Brandon, blond-haired and stocky with pale skin and freckles, lived just across the highway in the Brockland Apartments. His big brother, Steven, was getting a little too old to compete in the contests, but Brandon still liked getting the money. Two bucks was enough to buy some stuff at the Little Mac's store down the street.

He listened now to see what the next contest would be. He hoped it wouldn't be the old "Quiet Game" trick where the kid who stayed quiet the longest won. His grandfather didn't usually pull that one until the end of the day when he wanted to take a nap.

"OK," said Grandpa Willard, "I think we'll try bingo next. Maybe some of you older kids who've forgotten how to color can win at this. Never can tell. I'd hate to give away all my money to the little kids."

Grandpa Willard always kidded around like that. He liked telling jokes, especially ones that made Grandma Willard groan. Brandon liked hanging out at their house and playing with his twelve-year-old cousin, Melissa, who lived nearby. Some of his friends didn't like being around their relatives, but Brandon did. He got along pretty well with all his aunts and uncles and cousins. In fact, he got along with just about everybody—except, once in a while, with his parents.

He took a bingo card and balanced it on his knee as his grandfather pulled up the first number.

"B-4!"

Brandon searched his card but couldn't find a B-4. Chaz and Dustin, two of his cousins, moved little plastic bingo chips onto their cards. *Great,* Brandon thought. *I can't even win at bingo!*

"O-1!"

Brandon grinned; this time he had it. He used the tip of his finger to push a plastic red chip onto his card. A sideways glance told him nobody else had moved.

"N-14!"

"N-6!"

"G-21!"

As more and more spaces filled on everybody's cards, Brandon held his breath. Any second now, somebody was going to jump up and yell "BINGO!" He only had one more space to fill, the B-3. Come on, Grandpa, he thought, gimme a B-3.

Beethree, beeeee-threeee . . .

"B-3!"

"Yea-ah!" Brandon yelled. "I mean, bingo! I've got it! I won!"

Grandpa Willard pushed his glasses up higher on his nose. "Well, it's about time you won something. I thought I was going to have to cheat to make sure you got your two bucks. Here you go." Brandon laughed. "Thanks," he said, stuffing the money into his pants pocket. "If you want, though, you can cheat so I can win again."

Melissa reached over and popped Brandon on the side of the head. "I don't think so," she said. "*Some* of us still haven't won anything. If Grandpa's going to start cheating, he can cheat for me."

"Boy, you kids make it hard," said Grandpa Willard sadly. "And here I thought you were all such honest, upstanding citizens, too proud to accept help. I don't know . . . maybe I'd better stop these contests right now, before they get out of hand."

"Nooo!" the kids all chorused. "Do some more!"

The argument might have gone on longer if Brandon's mom, Debbie Skinner, hadn't stuck her head around the corner to announce: "Dinner's ready!" Bingo cards and plastic chips flew everywhere as the kids jumped up to stampede into the dining room, followed by Grandpa Willard and the various fathers and uncles who'd been watching the contests in amusement.

James Skinner, Brandon's stepdad, came up behind him. "Hey, pal," he said teasingly, "got a couple dollars I can borrow? I hear you're loaded."

Brandon grinned up at him. "Sorry, Dad, but I've already got plans. I may buy some beef jerky or licorice later." Mr. Skinner laughed and followed him into the dining room.

Thanksgiving Dinner

Brandon's mom had only married James Skinner that past January, but it seemed like he'd been part of their family for years. Brandon had never had trouble thinking of James as "Dad," since he always treated him like his own son. Brandon's natural father lived in Tennessee, so he didn't see him much. It was nice to have a dad around the house who could help him with homework and do stuff with him.

The huge Thanksgiving turkey was resting on a big platter beside Grandpa Willard's plate, ready to be carved. Brandon's mouth watered as he slid into a seat next to Dustin. Thanksgiving dinner was always the best meal of the year!

"OK, let's settle down now," said Grandpa Willard. "I'm going to offer thanks so we can start eating."

Brandon closed his eyes, hoping his grandfather would keep the prayer short. He could smell the warm turkey and sweet potato casserole. And the corn on the cob and the taco salad and the—

"Dear Lord," began Grandpa Willard humbly, "we want to give You thanks for this good meal and for all the family members around this table right now. Thank You for letting us be together on this fine day and for keeping us safe over this last year. In Jesus' name, amen."

Brandon opened his eyes and grabbed for the sweet potatoes in one movement. His mom gave him a reproachful look, but he pretended not to notice. He scooped a big spoonful of the potato-and-marshmallow mixture onto his plate, sucking a dab of marshmallow off his finger when it smeared.

Mm-mm, he thought happily. *Too bad Thanksgiving didn't happen every day.*

Steven nudged him. "Hey, after dinner you feel like going over to the park for a while? We can play football or something."

"OK. But I probably won't be able to run very fast." Brandon patted his stomach. "I'm planning to eat as much as I can."

"So what else is new?" Steven teased. He poked his brother's stomach with a sharp finger. "What is all that—Jell-O? Mush?"

"Steel," Brandon said. He was a *little* pudgy but not that much. He tightened his stomach and pounded it once or twice for effect. "Solid steel."

Steven laughed. "Smushiest steel I've ever felt. Maybe you'd better skip dessert tonight."

"No way!" Brandon exclaimed. "We're having chocolate pie, and lemon pie, and coconut pie . . . I might just have one of each!"

"In that case, you'd *better* come play football. Work some of it off."

After the turkey got hacked to pieces, and the bowls of sweet potatoes and cranberry sauce were scraped almost clean, Brandon leaned back in his chair with a sigh. About the only thing left on his plate was the broccoli—and he certainly wasn't in any hurry to get to that. He felt like he might explode if he ate any more, kind of like a human food bomb. Boom! Not a pretty picture.

Dustin and Melissa had excused themselves from the table a few minutes earlier. Now they appeared in the doorway. Melissa was tossing a football from hand to hand.

"You coming?" she asked. "Your brother said he'd play, too. He's on my team."

"I'm coming, I'm coming," Brandon said, prying himself up out of his chair. "But nobody better tackle me too hard. I ate too much."

"No joke," Melissa said, rubbing her own stomach. "I can hardly walk. This will be like slow-motion football."

"Turtle ball," Dustin said, giggling.

As the adults slowly stood up and started clearing the table, the kids all trooped outside. The park was just down the street. It didn't have a name, since it was mostly a big open field. Brandon and his best friend, Robert, often played there after school.

Robert, twelve, was in Brandon's sixth-grade class. They were built about the same—both a little chunky—but where Brandon was pale and blond, Robert, who was Hispanic, had dark skin, brown eyes, and curly black hair. Now, as Brandon reached the field with the others, he wished Robert would show up to join them. He was fast!

They ran and played for about an hour before deciding that it was time to head back for dessert. Maybe they'd worked off enough dinner to make room for pie. If not, they'd just have to force themselves.

Plowing into a thick slice of lemon pie a few minutes later, Brandon sighed happily. It had been a fun day, and it was just the first of the four-day holiday weekend. Best of all, it was only four more weeks until Christmas. He loved this time of year. Good food and lots of presents!

Brandon's family didn't go back home until almost six o'clock. It was hard to climb the stairs up to their second-story apartment in their condition. Brandon was tempted to get down on his hands and knees and crawl up.

"Well, did everybody have a good time?" asked Mr. Skinner, stifling a yawn. Eating a lot always made you feel sleepy, for some reason.

"I sure did," Brandon said, yawning back at him. "And I still have my two dollars for tomorrow."

"Yeah, it was fun," Steven said. "I'm going to go relax now and watch some TV. Let all that food settle."

Mrs. Skinner smiled. "Good idea."

The whole family lay around the living room like houseplants for a few hours and then one by one decided to call it a night.

Mr. Skinner stood up first. "Well, I'm going to bed," he said. "G'night everybody!"

"'Night, Dad," Steven said. "I think I'm going to head to bed, too." He stood up, stretched, and yawned loudly.

"I think we should all hit the sheets," Mrs. Skinner said. "Brandon, you ought to see yourself—you've got big dark circles under your eyes. They make you look like a raccoon."

"I'm going, I'm going," Brandon said. He followed Steven down the hall toward their room.

Brandon and Steven each had a single waterbed, neither one of which was made at the moment. Brandon pulled off his tennis shoes and kicked them toward the closet, and then peeled off his shirt and dropped it on the floor. Steven took off his baseball cap and glasses and tossed them onto the bedside stand.

"Today was fun," Steven said, stretching. "I hope Mom remembered to bring home some leftover turkey for tomorrow."

"Was there any pie left?"

Steven laughed. "I don't think so. If there was, Grandpa would have claimed it."

Brandon pulled on his pajamas and plopped down on the edge of his bed, making it slosh. "Well, I want to sleep late tomorrow," he said, riding the "waterbed wave." Lucky for him he didn't get seasick easy. "So don't wake me up."

"No problem. I'm planning to sleep in, too. Good night." Steven reached over to turn out the light.

"G'night," Brandon replied in the darkness. He rolled onto his side, pulled the sheet up to his neck and promptly fell asleep to dream about food and football.

A Fire-y Presentation

"Brandon?"

Brandon looked up with a start. His teacher, Mrs. Brown, was tapping her pencil on her grade book, waiting for him to call out how many math problems he'd missed. She had assigned twenty multiplication problems and then called out the answers so they could each grade their own papers. Math was Brandon's worst subject.

"Uh, I missed twr-mrm," he mumbled.

"I didn't hear that. How many?"

Brandon sighed. *What was the use?* "Twelve," he said clearly. "I missed twelve."

Someone behind snickered. He didn't look around. Mrs. Brown sighed. "I believe that gives you an 'F,' Mr. Abston," she said. "I think you'd better work harder on learning your multiplication tables."

"Yes'm, I'll try."

He was relieved when a loud siren suddenly wailed outside, distracting his classmates. Mrs. Brown had announced that morning that firefighters from Station #5 would be visiting the school that day. They must have just arrived.

"OK, class, settle down!" Mrs Brown exclaimed. "The sixth grade classes are going out first, so you need to line up quietly."

Brandon squeezed in toward the end of the line. At Mrs. Brown's signal, they all shuffled down the long hall and out through the front doors. Brandon waved when he spotted Robert shuffling outside with Mrs. Herbert's class.

The fire truck was parked along the curb. Three firefighters were standing in front of it, arms crossed, wearing fire suits with helmets, gloves, and heavy boots. Brandon stared at them enviously. Being a fireman must be a fun job.

Once all the classes were gathered, the firefighters walked back and forth shaking some of the kid's hands. Brandon pushed his way to the front of the crowd and was rewarded with a quick grasp from a gloved hand.

The men took turns explaining what all the things on the truck did and then led the way back inside to the cafeteria for a fire prevention talk. Brandon worked his way over to sit next to Robert. At least having real firemen there would be more interesting than the school's fire safety films.

The biggest fireman stood up. "Did you know that just last year, over thirty-five hundred people died in house fires?" he began. "And what makes that especially sad is that most of them would still be alive today if they had just taken a few simple precautions."

He looked around at the roomful of wriggling sixth-graders. "Now, all of you guys look pretty smart. I'll just bet you already know all about fire safety, don't you?"

"Yeah!" chorused a handful of kids. Brandon grinned and nudged Robert. It was probably going to be another "Stop-Drop-and-Roll" speech, but it was still better than math.

The fireman nodded. "Well, then why don't we have a little quiz? I would like for a couple of you guys who know all about fires to come on up here and help me."

Two boys from Mrs. Herbert's class jumped up and went to the front. The fireman stood next to them. "OK," he said. "Here's your first question: How do fires kill most people?"

The boy to his right giggled. "That's easy," he said. "It burns them up!"

The fireman shook his head. "Sorry, that's not correct. Smoke usually kills people before the flames ever reach them."

The boy looked embarrassed. "Oh."

"Here, I'll give you guys another chance," the fireman said kindly. "What should you do if you're helping your mom fry some chicken or something, and the skillet catches on fire?"

The boy who had answered before kept his mouth shut and let his friend answer this time. "Put it in the sink and pour water on it?"

"You're wrong again. You never, ever put water on a grease fire. All that will do is spread the flames. You should put a lid over the skillet to cut off the oxygen and then turn off the burner. A fire won't keep burning without oxygen."

He looked down and smiled. "Hey, I thought you guys knew all about fires. What's the problem?"

"I guess we didn't know everything," the first boy said as he went to sit down. "We just know that you're supposed to stop, drop, and roll if your clothes catch on fire, and to feel doors to see if they're hot before you open them. Stuff like that."

The fireman nodded. "Well, that's a good start. But did you know that burning carpet and paint, and even some kinds of couch cushions can create poisonous gases? That's why it's so important, if you're ever in a fire, to stay down low, where the air is clearer. It doesn't take much smoke to do you in."

Brandon listened carefully as the man went over prevention tips and then the survival rules: Stay calm. Alert everybody. Crawl to safety. Get out as fast as you can. Never go back into a burning building.

Brandon was sorry when it was over. Back in class, he kept thinking how exciting it would be to be a fireman. Maybe that's what he should be when he grew up.

With a sigh, he turned back to his math book. *That's another good thing about being a fireman,* he thought. *They didn't have to do a lot of stupid old math!*

Not Just an Ordinary Day

"Robert!"

It was Wednesday afternoon the following week. Brandon yelled his friend's name and then kicked the soccer ball toward him, trying to shoot it past Gilbert and Paul. The open courtyard in the middle of the Brockland Apartments made a good soccer field. Two of the tall brick units faced each other, and the walls stopped the ball before it could roll too far out of bounds.

Robert got the ball and started dribbling toward the "goal," a wooden privacy fence. Before he could shoot, though, one of the other kids stole it and charged off in the other direction. Brandon took off after him.

"Braan-don!" The voice could barely be heard over their excited shouts. "Dinnertime!"

Brandon skidded to a halt. His family's apartment was in the building to the right, and their kitchen window faced the courtyard. His mom was standing at the window waving a "come home" signal.

"I've gotta go, guys," he said breathlessly. "My grandma and grandpa are here for dinner tonight, and my mom'll kill me if I don't get right up there."

Robert, his face flushed, trotted up and stopped. "I think I'll go home, too," he said. "Come on, I'll walk with you."

They'd only taken a few steps toward the apartment building, though, when Brandon suddenly yelled, "Hey! Look at that!"

Robert followed his gaze. The windows of a ground floor apartment directly ahead were filled with huge orange flames! As they stared, black smoke poured from the windows and out from under the front door.

Brandon acted quickly. "*FIRE!*" he yelled. "Fire! Fire!" Then he turned to shout back to their other friends: "Call 9-1-1!" Heart pounding, he raced forward, Robert at his heels. What if somebody was inside the burning apartment?

Reaching the door, he put his fists up to pound on it. That was when he heard the muffled screams from inside.

"Help! Help!" It was a child's faint cry, almost a sob. Brandon felt his throat tighten with fear. A kid was inside there! He looked around wildly, but there was no one else to help. He turned to Robert.

"I'm going inside. You stay here and show the firemen where to go when they show up."

"You can't go in there!" Robert cried. He grabbed Brandon's arm. "You'll fry!"

"A little kid's in there!" Shaking his friend off, Brandon turned the doorknob and found it was unlocked. He shoved it open and darted inside.

He hadn't even taken one step, though, before a thick, choking cloud of smoke billowed up around his face. The entire living room ceiling was boiling with flames. Even the overhead light was on fire! Coughing, eyes stinging, Brandon dropped to his hands and knees. The air would be better down by the floor.

He could now hear the childish screams for help more clearly. It sounded like there was more than one! He looked around in a panic. The smoke was so thick he could hardly see in front of his face.

"Where are you?" he shouted. "Yell so I can hear you!"

It was hard to hear anything over the roaring flames above. The children cried out again and Brandon started crawling toward the sound of their voices. The apartment seemed to be laid out exactly like his; if so, the kids were probably back in the smaller of the two bedrooms.

"Keep yelling!"

Off to his left, in the kitchen, all the cabinets and countertops were on fire. Huge flames poured out of the kitchen into the living room. It looked like the fire might have started in there. Maybe it hadn't reached the back bedrooms yet!

Keeping his body low, trying not to breathe the smoke, Brandon crawled back to the smaller bedroom. It was filled with smoke, but no flames had reached it.

"Are you in here?" he yelled. "Where are you?" There was no answer. The children must be in the other, larger bedroom. He crawled back out into the hallway and felt his way along the wall until he reached the master bedroom. He crawled inside the room and glanced around, but he still didn't see anybody.

"Where are you?" he yelled. "Answer me!"

Fear and Fire

"We're behind the bed!" a young voice wailed. Brandon quickly scrambled around the end of the bed. Sure enough, the sobbing children were huddled there in a frightened heap—*four* of them! The oldest child, a boy about five, was holding a baby on his lap; beside him, two little girls about two and three years old clung to him, their eyes wide with fear. Brandon crawled to their sides.

"Come on!" he said, tugging at the older boy's arm. "You've got to get out of here!"

The boy shrank away from him, holding the baby tightly. "No!" he said in an odd, hesitant voice. "Mama . . . said not . . . to go."

Brandon stared, suddenly recognizing the small boy. His name, he remembered vaguely, was Michael something. Brandon had seen him around the apartments a few times with his little sisters. He seemed to be mildly retarded.

"You've *got* to!" Brandon said firmly. "You'll burn up if you don't! Come on!" The boy still stubbornly shook his head. Brandon made a decision.

"Give me the baby!" he ordered. "I'm taking her out of here!"

"*No!*" The frightened boy began to kick and flail as Brandon pried his hands off the infant. Brandon was finally able to jerk the baby free and he hugged her close.

"Ya'll stay here!" he said. "I'll be right back!" Tucking the baby up close to his neck, he dashed, bent over, back out toward the hallway.

As he made his way back out to the living room, Brandon saw that the fire was now creeping down the walls toward the furniture. Through the thick smoke he saw a hanging plant and a picture in flames. Two big spots on the carpet were also burning. Coughing and gagging, he dodged his way past the flames to reach the apartment door.

Robert was standing just outside, surrounded by a crowd of both kids and adults. When Brandon staggered out, he shoved the baby into his friend's arms. The whole courtyard was now hazy with smoke from the burning apartment.

"There are three other kids in there!" Brandon gasped, trying to catch his breath. "I've got to go back in!"

"You can't!" Robert pleaded. "Wait for the firemen!"

"It might be too late by then." Brandon glanced around, half-hoping one of the adults would step forward to help. None of them did. Scared and a little angry, he wheeled around and plunged back into the apartment.

The black smoke made his eyes sting as he groped his way back to the master bedroom again. The flames overhead had crept farther back along the ceiling. Now they were licking in through the top of the bedroom door. It wouldn't be long before the whole bedroom caught on fire.

He scrambled over to where the kids were sitting. The tiny girls were both hanging onto their big brother, sobbing.

Brandon decided to take the two-year-old next. "OK, you're coming with me," he said, scooping her up before her brother could get a good grip on her.

"No!" she shrieked. As she twisted and squirmed, trying to wriggle out of his arms, the other two kids hit and clawed at Brandon. He almost dropped the toddler when her brother's fist slammed into the side of his head.

"You can't stay in here!" Brandon said angrily. "You'll all fry! Now leave me alone."

When he carried the little girl, kicking and screaming, out into the hallway, he saw that the flames had spread most of the way across the living room carpet.

The mini-blinds on the front window were on fire, and the couch was smoldering. Brandon remembered what the fireman at his school had said about burning couch cushions making poison gas. There were flames above, flames below—and deadly smoke in the middle. He pressed his lips together, trying not to breathe. He knew enough about fire to know that people often died from smoke before flames could even reach them.

Carrying the squirming toddler sideways in his arms, he hunched over and dashed toward the door. He zigzagged, trying to step on the few parts of the carpet that weren't burning yet, but even so, the smoke got to him. He started coughing so hard that he thought he was going to throw up. He barely made it to the door.

Stumbling outside, he dropped the little girl and then remained bent over, coughing and gagging, his eyes streaming with tears. Even the smoky air outside was a relief to his aching lungs.

Robert stood over him, worried. "Hey, Brandon, are you OK?" He patted his friend's back, trying to help him breathe.

The crowd outside had now grown to over twenty people. One lady was holding the baby Brandon had brought out first; another one now moved forward to comfort the child he'd just brought out. The rest of them, including three or four men, just stood there watching. Robert was angry. *What is wrong with them? Why don't one of them volunteer?*

Two More Still Inside

Brandon stayed bent over, his hands propped on his knees. He stared down at his pants legs, surprised to see how black they were. It must be soot from all the smoke, he thought dizzily. His hands were black and sticky, too. That was probably why he was coughing so hard—his lungs were coated with the stuff. That wasn't good.

He spat on the ground, trying to get the sickening taste out of his mouth, and then stood up shakily. "I'm OK," he said. "But there are two more kids in there."

"Don't be dumb, Brandon. The whole place is on fire now. Wait for the firemen!"

Brandon hesitated. Robert was right; it was stupid to go back inside. It wouldn't help anybody if he died in there. But he didn't even hear fire engine sirens yet. If the firemen didn't get there soon, the two kids left inside would suffocate from the smoke. "I've got to try one more time," Brandon said. "I'll be careful."

He took several deep breaths, trying to store up as much oxygen as he could. Then he ran back into the flaming apartment. Squinting his eyes against the hot smoke, he charged straight back to the bedroom, holding his breath the whole way. He hoped the air in the bedroom would be better.

But in the few seconds he'd spent outside, the fire had spread. Now the bedroom, too, was thick with smoke. Panic gripped Brandon as he burst into the room. He needed *air!*

Bending down low, he pulled his shirt up to cover his nose and mouth. He breathed through the fabric, hoping that it would filtering out some of the smoke. There wasn't a minute to lose. He had to get those last two kids out before the whole place turned into a fireball.

The boy and girl were still sitting in the same place, kind of hiding behind the bed. What did they think, that they could hide from the flames? Brandon decided not to waste his breath by talking any more. He just crawled over and grabbed the little girl, ignoring her brother's stammered protests.

But the three-year-old was bigger—and heavier—than either of her younger sisters. As Brandon hauled her, kicking and wailing, toward the bedroom door, he was suddenly afraid. What if he took her out into the living room and she ended up dying from all the smoke? She needed to hold her breath, but he didn't think she would listen to him. His best bet was to get her out quick, before she had time to breathe too much smoke.

Please let us get out of here, he prayed with a pounding heart. *Please don't let me drop her or get turned around.*

The living room walls and ceiling were all black and melted-looking now, the carpet a sea of flames. The couch was on fire now too, adding to the choking smoke. Brandon remembered again that the smoke from couch cushions was poisonous. He pressed his lips together tighter and bent as low as he could before dashing into the living room, aiming—he hoped—for the front door.

He had only taken a few steps when he felt the little girl in his arms stiffen and then start choking and gagging. He kept going. There was nothing he could do to help. Sweat ran down his face, leaving dirty black streaks as he raced on blindly through the smoke and flames, hoping he was still going in the right direction. He hardly noticed the pain in his leg as he banged into the sharp corner of the coffee table. The wooden legs were charred black and starting to burn.

It seemed, in his panic, to take forever to reach the front door. When he finally staggered outside, Robert whisked the little girl from his arms and handed her to another adult in the crowd.

Brandon gasped. "There's just one more. A boy."

Robert had his arm around Brandon's shoulder, helping hold him up. "You're not going back in there," Robert said firmly. "The fire department's almost here. Hear the sirens?"

Sure enough, sirens were wailing in the distance. He let himself relax a little. He didn't have to go back. The firemen would come with their fire truck, water hoses, and fire suits and get the little boy out. He could just stand there, nice and safe, and watch with the rest of the crowd.

Running Out of Time

But at that moment, a woman pushed her way through the crowd carrying a grocery bag. When she reached the apartment door and saw the roaring fire inside, she dropped her groceries on the concrete. The bag burst, sending a can of peas rolling across the pavement and into the grass.

"My kids!" she screamed. "That's my apartment. My kids are in there!"

A woman in the crowd pointed at Brandon. "He got three out already. A baby and two girls."

The hysterical mother looked over at Brandon, her eyes dark with despair. "My son!" she said. "I've got to get my son out! He won't know what to do!"

Brandon stared at her, seeing the unspoken plea in her face. "I'll go back in and get him," he said.

Robert exploded. "No, you won't!" He pounced on Brandon from behind, wrapping his arms around his friend's chest. "You're gonna stay right here. Don't even think about it."

"Let me go, Robert!" With a burst of strength, Brandon broke away. Before Robert could grab him again, he ran back into the burning apartment.

The crowd gasped as Brandon disappeared into the orange-red flames. "He's going to be killed!" a man yelled. A woman started crying. The children's mother stood there, moaning and sobbing, "Oh, no. Oh, no!"

Inside, Brandon was feeling more scared than he'd ever been in his life. The whole living room was now on fire—the carpet, the walls, the furniture, even the air. Flames boiled all around him, and the thick black smoke blinded him. After only a moment's hesitation he dived for the only flame-free area, a small pocket of smoky air low in the center of the room.

Doubled over, holding his breath, he dashed back toward where the child was trapped. Over the noisy roar of the flames he could hear the little boy screaming and choking. Had the fire already reached him?

If so, I'm dead, Brandon thought. *I'll never get back out before I have to take another breath. If the whole bedroom is on fire it's all over.* He reached the bedroom door and felt his way inside, relieved to see that the flames along the ceiling hadn't caught the bed on fire—yet. He took a shallow breath, but it made him cough. Still choking, he ran around the bed to the little boy.

But when he tried to make him get up, the child still slapped and kicked at him. Even with his sisters gone, he was afraid to leave.

Brandon didn't want to waste any time. He scooped the boy up off the floor and held him pinned tightly in his arms. Still, when the child started twisting and squirming, Brandon almost dropped him. It was like trying to hang onto a mad tiger.

I can't do this, Brandon thought, turning his face away to keep from getting slapped again. *He's too big for me.*

But what other choice did he have? It wasn't the kid's fault that he didn't understand what was going on. Brandon couldn't just dump him and leave him to burn.

Squashing the boy's body even harder against his chest, Brandon crouched down again and started back toward the living room. He could hardly walk, much less run, carrying the child's added weight, but somehow he had to make it through those flames. If he didn't . . .

Don't think about it, Brandon told himself. *Just do it. Just do it!*

The pocket of air near the living room floor was much smaller now, barely big enough for Brandon, bent over, to fit through. The fiery air above him roared and swirled like a blowtorch; the flames from the carpet licked up around his ankles. If he stood up straight, his head and shoulders would be engulfed in fire.

The apartment door was just ahead.

Gathering up the last bit of his rapidly fading strength, Brandon launched himself forward. He tumbled onto the concrete outside at Robert's feet, coughing and gasping.

"Brandon!" Robert yelled with relief. "You made it! You did it!"

The boy's mother ran over and grabbed her son, hugging him thankfully. "Thank you!" she said hysterically. "Thank you!"

Brandon was coughing too hard to answer. He nodded shakily as if to say, "That's OK."

The fire trucks began pulling into the apartment complex. Brandon slowly caught his breath and then watched as the firefighters ran up, unrolling a flat fire hose. The crowd backed into the courtyard to watch.

Brandon glanced up at the apartments above them. "We've got to get everybody out of the building," he told Robert. "The fire might spread. I'll run upstairs and tell my mom and the others on the second floor." Robert nodded. "And I'll go this way," he pointed to the right, "and make sure everybody on the bottom's out. If they're not," he added, "they must be deaf."

Brandon ran for the stairs. A moment later, he burst in through the front door of his family's apartment, almost running right into his mother. She stared at him as he skidded to a stop.

"Brandon Abston, what on earth have you done to yourself?" she exclaimed. "You're black all over! And just look at your clothes—"

"Mom! Forget my clothes. You've got to get out of here! There's a fire downstairs!"

"A fire?" Mrs. Skinner looked at him suspiciously. "Brandon, if there's a fire, don't you go anywhere near it, you hear me?"

"Uh," Brandon said. "Uh, well, I've got to go tell everybody else up here to get out, too. I'll find you outside, OK?"

"OK. But you remember what I said. Fires are dangerous!"

"Yeah. See you outside."

A moment later, running from apartment to apartment, Brandon banged hard on each door and yelled, "Fire!" at the top of his lungs. People started pouring out into the hallway and heading for the stairs.

Young Hero

Finally, after he'd banged on every door, Brandon went down to join his family. It looked like everybody in the whole apartment complex was standing out in the courtyard now, watching the firefighters at work. Through the windows he could see several of them spraying down the kitchen.

Grandma and Grandpa Willard looked up as Brandon approached. "Hoo, boy, are you a mess," said Grandpa Willard. "What've you been doing, rolling in coal dust? Even your hair is black."

Brandon ran a hand through his blond hair, but his fingers came away black and greasy. He wrinkled his nose. "Well," he said, "I—"

Just then, Robert came running up. "Brandon! Did you tell your mom and dad what you did?"

Brandon tried to shush him, but Robert didn't pay any attention.

"You should have seen him, Mrs. Skinner!" he exclaimed. "He saved four little kids' lives! He ran right into the fire and brought them out, one by one. He's a hero!"

Mr. and Mrs. Skinner, Steven, and Grandma and Grandpa Willard all turned to stare at Brandon, their mouths forming little "O's."

"You did *what?*" Mrs. Skinner sputtered in disbelief.

"I was kind of the first one to see the fire," Brandon explained uncomfortably, "and then, when I went to bang on the door, I heard these little kids inside crying and screaming." He looked at his mom steadily. "I couldn't just stand there and let them burn, could I?"

Mrs. Skinner was still trying to take it all in when Robert spoke again.

"There were a bunch of grown-ups standing around watching the whole time, but they were all too scared to help. Brandon did it all by himself. Those kids would've been toast if he hadn't dragged them out."

Mr. Skinner shook his head in disbelief. "Our son, the hero," he said softly, putting his arm around Brandon's shoulders. "I'm proud of you, son."

Grandpa Willard patted Brandon on the arm, not caring that his hand came away black with soot. "It took a lot of courage, to do that," he said.

"It wasn't that big a deal," Brandon lied.

Mrs. Skinner finally snapped out of her shock. "Oh, yes, it was!" she said. "I don't know whether to kiss you or kick you, young man. You could have been killed!"

"But I wasn't," Brandon reminded her. "See?" He waved his arms in the air a few times to demonstrate his aliveness, hoping to make her laugh. It worked.

"You're a mess," Mrs. Skinner said, ruffling his dirty hair. "You need a bath. But first I want to talk to the firemen and find out if you need to get checked out at the hospital."

"Oh, Mom!" Brandon said in exasperation. "I'm OK. I don't need any hospital."

After the fire was put out, Mrs. Skinner took Brandon over to one of the firefighters and explained what he had done. The man grinned down at Brandon.

"We heard all about you," he said. "Sounds like you had everything taken care of before we got here. But what you did was dangerous, you know. Going into a burning building is something firemen are trained for, but we have special suits and oxygen masks." He patted Brandon's shoulder. "You ever think about being a firefighter when you grow up?"

Brandon grinned back at him. "Yeah. I think I'd like that."

Since Brandon was breathing OK and didn't have any serious burns, the firefighter thought it would be OK for him to just go home and take a bath.

"Not that you *need* one," he added with a smile. Brandon laughed.

The next morning, Brandon read in the newspaper that the fire had started from a pot on the stove that had suddenly burst into flames. The whole kitchen had burned away to almost nothing.

"I thought it must've started there," Brandon said. "When I first went in, big flames were coming from the kitchen."

A few weeks later, over Christmas break, Brandon received an invitation from the fire chief to be a "Fireman for a Day." He got to spend the night at the local station, where he was issued his own firefighter uniform: a helmet, jacket, pants, and boots. When "his" truck was called out to a car wreck, he rode along with the other firemen. It was the most exciting night he'd ever spent in his life. He decided for sure that he wanted to be a firefighter someday.

The city council in Lawton also presented him with two plaques honoring him for his heroism. Brandon wasn't quite sure what to say, though, when they asked him what it had been like. He'd had a lot of nightmares for a few weeks about being trapped in a fire. He kept waking up sweaty and screaming, his heart pounding with fear. The truth was, he hadn't felt at all heroic that day in the burning apartment. He'd felt scared to death!

But his dad said that was OK. "Real courage isn't about not being scared," he told him. "It's about what you do when you *are* scared.

"You ignored your own fear that day to go help somebody else who needed it . . . and in my book, Brandon, that's what courage is all about."

Do You Have a Real Kids, Real Adventures Story?

We're looking for TRUE stories for future volumes of *Real Kids, Real Adventures*—stories about real kids ages nine to seventeen who have faced danger or crisis with extraordinary courage or sometimes become real life heroes. If you have heard about such a story, we might like to use it. The first person to submit a story that we use will have his or her name mentioned in the book and will receive a free copy of that book when it is published.

Please send your story ideas to: Real Kids, Real Adventures, P.O. Box 461572, Garland TX 75046-1572. Please include your name, address, phone number with area code, and a newspaper clipping with the name and date of the paper, and/or factual information we can use to research the story.

///